CW01627524

THE ENCHANTMENT OF THE TROSSACHS

The Story of Robert Kirk

Louis Stott

2018

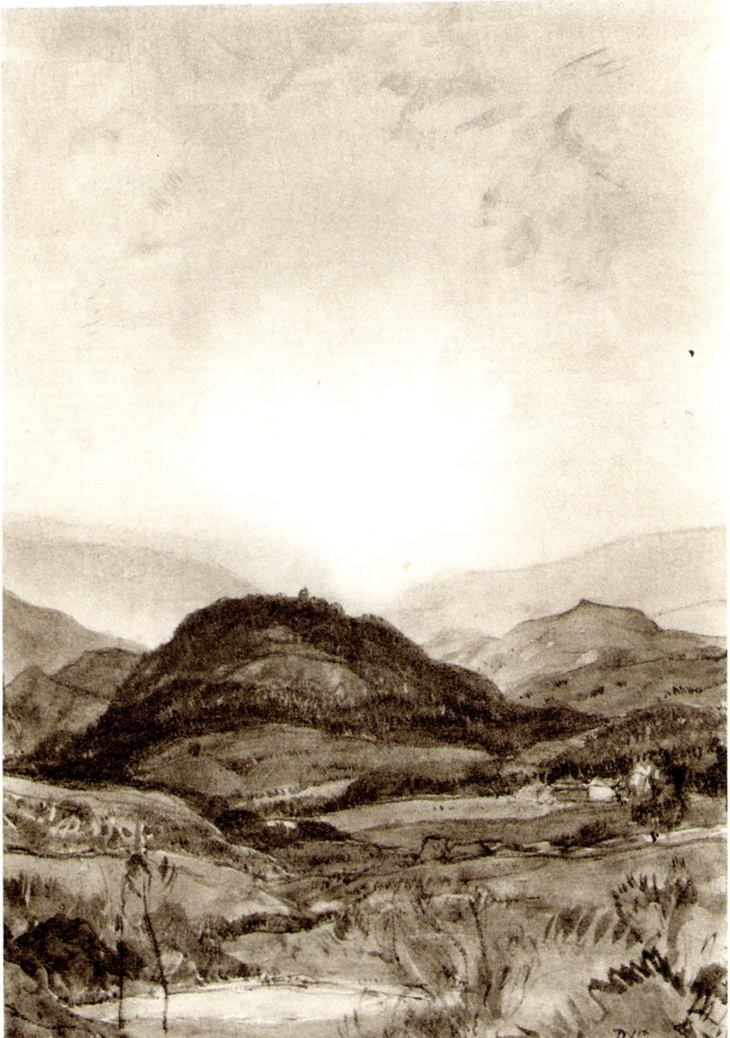

THE HILL OF THE FAIRIES AT ABERFOYLE

From a Watercolour Drawing by Sir D. Y. Cameron, R.A.

© Louis Stott
2018

Revised Edition

Published By
Loch Ard Local History Group
Kinlochard, FK8 3TL

Loch Ard Local History Group gratefully acknowledges the financial assistance of: The Strathard Initiative; The Friends of OUR Park Visitor Giving Scheme; The Aberfoyle Business Partnership.

Every effort has been made to trace the copyright holders of the images used. Where this has not been possible the publishers would appreciate any up-to-date information on inadvertent omissions.

Cover Design: Katinka Dalglish

ISBN: 978-1-9999487-0-2
Printed by Soapbox Design & Print Glasgow

Dedication

For Valentino Smith

Acknowledgements

The author gratefully acknowledges and commends previous workers in the field, particularly undertakings by authors listed in the bibliography. Illustrations in the text are from the author's collection, except where otherwise acknowledged. The author is particularly indebted to Alan Cooper and Bernard Love for local photographs, and to Katinka Dalglish for designing the cover. The frontispiece is from a watercolour drawing by D. Y. Cameron which was used to illustrate Cunninghame Graham's edition of Kirk's *Secret Commonwealth*. The kindness of the *Loch Ard Local History Group* in undertaking the publication of the second edition of this work is greatly appreciated, particularly the efforts of its Chairman, James Kennedy and of Catherine Love, the copy editor.

The Fairy Minister

The Rev. Mr Kirk of Aberfoyle was carried away by the Fairies in 1692

People of Peace! a peaceful man,
Well worthy of your love was he,
Who, while the roaring Garry ran
Red with the lifeblood of Dundee,
While coats were turning, crowns were falling,
Wandered along his valley still,
And heard your mystic voices calling
From fairy knowe and haunted hill.
He heard, he saw, he knew too well
The secrets of your fairy clan;
You stole him from the haunted dell,
Who never more was seen of man.
Now far from heaven, and safe from hell,
Unknown of earth he wanders free.
Would that he might return and tell
Of his mysterious Company!
For we have tired the Folk of Peace;
No more they tax our corn and oil;
Their dances on the moorland cease,
The Brownie stints his wonted toil.
No more shall any shepherd meet
The ladies of the fairy clan,
Nor are their deathly kisses sweet
On lips of any earthly man.
And half I envy him who now,
Clothed in her Court's enchanted green,
By moonlit loch or mountain's brow,
Is Chaplain to the Fairy Queen.

Andrew Lang *Ban and Arrière Ban* 1894

THE ENCHANTMENT OF THE TROSSACHS

The Story of Robert Kirk

"In a century like our own, multifariously occupied with trivialities and so highly charged with shattering possibilities, one may profitably inquire what latent quality in at least some of us stimulates, from time to time, a meticulous re-appraisal of the beliefs and performances of our forefathers. It may well be a deep-seated awareness that even matters of Fairie, being less disturbing than those of nuclear physics, tend to provide a modicum of balance and sanity in an age that has already demonstrated, pretty conclusively, its ability to obliterate itself."

Alasdair Alpin MacGregor *Land of the Mountain and the Flood* 1965

If Loch Ness has a corner in water monsters, and the Cairngorms have a monopoly of mountain apparitions, the Trossachs in general, and Aberfoyle in particular, enjoy – in Scotland at least – an unrivalled reputation for fairies. Aberfoyle is the fairy capital of Scotland because the Reverend Robert Kirk, minister of the parish, ended his days there in close touch, it is said, with fairyland. In the second decade of the twenty-first century this proposition may be regarded as absurd, and it must be asserted that there is less interest in fairies nowadays than there was in the seventeenth century. Robert Kirk might be perceived, on this account, as a figure of fun, and receive less attention than he deserves. However, in considering his life and its influence, it is essential to recollect that, until very recently, superstition played an important part in country life. Indeed, it could be argued that it still does, but much that was then unexplained made sense if you involved fairies.

Superstition is unfashionable. The language has, regrettably, abused words which, once upon a time, were to be taken seriously, or, at least, conjured up widely-respected images. Folklore, primitive beliefs, pagan rituals, religion, the dead, changelings, household spirits, and fairies were formerly intermingled in people's minds. They represent the roots of our society. Nowadays legends are regarded as interesting – providing they are not too fantastic; religion is respectable, but the occult is not; and fairies are no longer taken seriously. At the edge of the Highlands such distinctions were much more blurred until less than a hundred years ago.

Robert Kirk (1644–92) was the Minister of the Parish of Aberfoyle from 1685 to 1692. Like many ministers he was a noted scholar who, among his other achievements, was the first to translate the Metrical Psalms into Gaelic, and he was asked to superintend the publication of the most significant Gaelic Bible of the seventeenth century. However, it was his interest in fairies, and his publication of *The Secret Commonwealth*, the book about Scottish fairies, which gave him a lasting reputation. **Walter Scott**, the distinguished writer and poet, stated that he had never seen a printed version of the 1691 edition of this book, but it has survived, and there are still current editions of it. It has interested and inspired other writers, better known than Kirk, in various ways. Scott edited an edition in 1815; **Andrew Lang**, the folklorist and poet, edited the next version in 1893; and **Robert Bontine Cunninghame Graham**, the most important writer who resided in the district, contributed to a third edition in 1933, which was illustrated by **David Young Cameron**, the eminent painter. The text used for these editions is regarded as unreliable, although they are of considerable literary interest. In 1976, **Stewart Sanderson**, Professor of Dialect and Folk Life Studies at the University of Leeds, produced a revised version of the text from the original manuscripts in the National Library and Edinburgh University Library with a new introduction and commentary. An edition in modern English by **R. J. Stewart** was published in 1990, and there are numerous others.

*

Kirk's birth date is often given as 1641, making his age 51 years when he was supposedly carried off by the fairies. However, Stewart Sanderson, one of the most notable modern scholars to have investigated Kirk, gives his date of birth as 9 December 1644. He was the seventh and youngest son of **James Kirk** (d.1658), minister at Aberfoyle, and his wife, **Elizabeth Carkettle** (d.1679) of Edinburgh. Kirk studied at Edinburgh University (where he graduated MA on 19 July 1661), and at St Andrews. On 8 November 1664 he became the minister of Balquhidder, Perthshire, and from 23 October 1667 to 3 April 1688 he was the reliable and well-regarded clerk to the Synod of Dunblane. From 1660 to 1671 the Bishop of Dunblane was **Robert Leighton**.

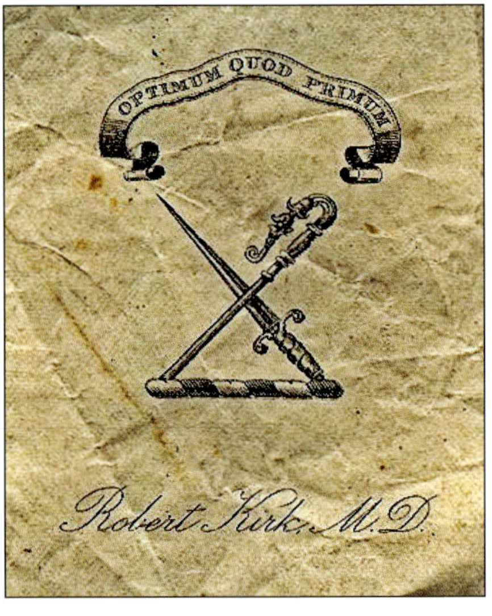

Robert Kirk's Coat of Arms

Kirk's lifetime was a period of exceptional political and religious upheaval in Scotland: when he was four Charles I, who sought to impose both Bishops and an alien Prayer Book on Scotland, was executed; and when he was nine, Cromwell's troops, who eventually subdued the whole of Scotland, were defeated in the Pass of Aberfoyle. He lived to see the Restoration of Charles II, both in Scotland and in England, the reign of his Roman Catholic brother, James II and VII, and the revolutionary succession of William of Orange. He took the oath imposed by the Test Act of 1681. Kirk was an Episcopalian and during much of his ministry Episcopalianism was imposed upon Scotland, but Presbyterianism was restored in 1688. Kirk survived these changes, but some of his colleagues were driven from their pulpits, persecuted and killed for their beliefs.

On 14 January 1678 Kirk married Isabel, daughter of Sir Colin Campbell of Mochaster (1616–68) and Margaret Menzies (d. 1681). They had two sons, Colin (d. 1725), who eventually became a writer to the signet in Edinburgh, and William, who died an infant. Isabel died on 25 December 1680, aged twenty-five, and was buried at Balquhidder; Kirk himself cut the epitaph on her gravestone.

When James Kirk died he was succeeded by the inept Daniel McVicar, but in 1685 Kirk took his father's charge at Aberfoyle. He married again, and a son, Robert (d. 1758) who became minister of Dornoch, was born about 1690. His second wife, Margaret Campbell of Fordie, was a cousin of his first wife. Margaret was pregnant with their second child, Marjorie, when Kirk died at Aberfoyle on 14 May 1692. He is buried in the old kirkyard there.

Kirk is a highly significant figure. Perhaps his greatest achievement in his own lifetime was to make the Bible accessible in the Highlands of Scotland during these troubled times when even the inhabitants of the parish of Aberfoyle were overwhelmingly Gaelic speakers. An Irish version had been available for some years and it provided the basis for the transliteration which the redoubtable minister then went to London to see through the press. Kirk's Bible was in use for over a hundred years. However, alongside these labours, Kirk collected local folk tales, and made one of the first scientific studies of the supernatural.

*

Kirk's interest in fairies ought to be granted more respectability than it sometimes is. Perhaps it would be if his death had not given rise to a curious and dramatic legend: his spiriting away by the fairies, and his re-appearance as a wraith. This story was – quite rightly – emphatically dismissed by his principal biographer, **Reverend Professor Donald Maclean** (1869–1943), in a paper given to the Gaelic Society of Inverness in 1924, but, despite such strictures, it has persisted. It was revitalised by the interest taken in 'close encounters of the third kind', and in pagan beliefs, as an aspect of what has been called the 'New Age.' These pseudo-scientific connections distance the scientific community from Kirk, and result in him being regarded as a figure of fun.

It was Kirk's habit to go every day to Doon Hill, the fairy knoll behind the old parish church. His death occurred on the hill on 14 May 1692. It is probable that he had a heart attack as a result of exertions, but it was said locally that the fairies had spirited him away because he had published his book revealing their secrets, and that they had substituted a stock, a changeling. This explains how Kirk can be buried in the old graveyard, but could, at the same time, be in fairyland. Indeed, it has long been said that the Minister of

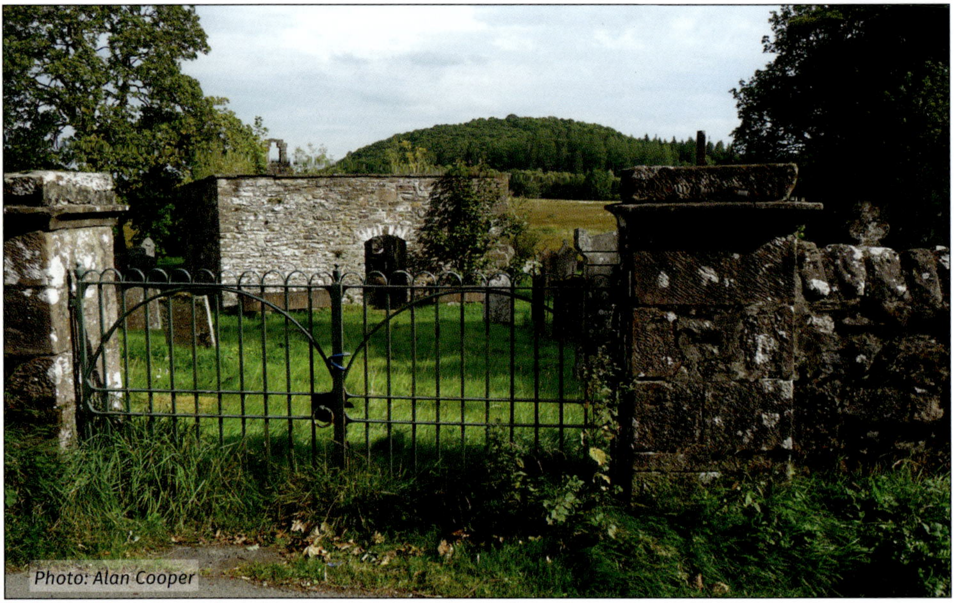

Doon Hill from the Kirkyard

the Parish continues to be Kirk; and that his successors are merely standing in for him. **Patrick Graham**, one of Kirk's successors as minister of the parish, outlines the curious occurrence after his death:

> "Mr Kirk was the near relation of Graham of Duchray, the ancestor of the present General Graham. Shortly after his funeral he appeared in the dress in which he had sunk down, to a medical relation of his own, and of Duchray. 'Go,' said he to him, 'to my cousin Duchray and tell him I am not dead. I fell down in a swoon, and was carried away into fairyland, where I now am. Tell him, that when he and my friends are assembled at the baptism of my child (for he had left his wife pregnant), I will appear in the room, and that if he throws the knife which he holds in his hand over my head, I will be released, and restored to human society.' The man, it seems, neglected for some time, to deliver the message. Mr Kirk appeared to him a second time, threatening to haunt him night and day until he executed his commission, which at length he did. The time of the baptism arrived. They were seated at the table; the figure of Mr Kirk entered, but the laird of Duchray, by some unaccountable fatality, neglected to perform the prescribed ceremony. Mr Kirk retired by another door, and was seen no more. It is firmly believed that he is, at this day, in fairyland."

Patrick Graham *Sketches of Perthshire* 1812

This tradition was still very much alive more than a hundred years after Patrick Graham's death. **Walter Evans-Wentz** (1878–1965), the American folklorist, found it to be current when he investigated *The Fairy Faith in Celtic Countries* in Aberfoyle in 1908. **Lewis Spence** (1874–1955), and **Katharine Briggs** (1898–1980) added to the tradition (*see below*).

It is rather more surprising, although it does add a further element of intrigue to the story of Robert Kirk, that the dates of Kirk's birth and of his death should be the subject of so much confusion. Scott, relying on Patrick Graham, asserts that he died in 1688 at the age of forty-two. This would fix the date of his birth in 1646. It is obviously wrong, because Kirk went to London in 1689 (perhaps considered locally to be the equivalent of death), completed his transliteration of the *Bible* in 1690, and almost certainly wrote The *Secret Commonwealth* after that. Others, including Hew Scott in his *Fasti*, the catalogue of Ministers of the Parishes in Scotland, and Andrew Lang, assert that he was fifty-one – or in his fifty-second year – when he died in 1692, making his birth date 1641. Kirk himself left in a notebook the information that he was 45 in December 1689 (that is, he was born in 1644), and, although this would make him less than twenty when he became the Minister of Balquhidder in November 1664, it is the date which his most reliable biographers accept. Kirk's grave is in the old kirkyard in the Kirkton, Aberfoyle. It would have been hard under the eaves of the kirk, now roofless.

It is a red-sandstone slab which is raised from the ground by another slab which bears the date, 1793. Stewart Sanderson states that it 'is almost certainly not contemporary. The style of the lettering suggests the end of the 18th century, or later'. The present stone was almost certainly reworked during the incumbency of the Reverend William Taylor. The gravestone is inscribed with a coat of arms, a thistle and crossed sword and crozier, and with the following inscription:

HIC SEPULTUS
ILLE EVANGELLI
PROMULGATOR
ACCURATUS
ET
LINGUAE HIBERNIAE
LUMEN
M. ROBERTUS KIRK
ABERFOILE PASTOR
OBIIT 14 MAII 1692
AETAT 48

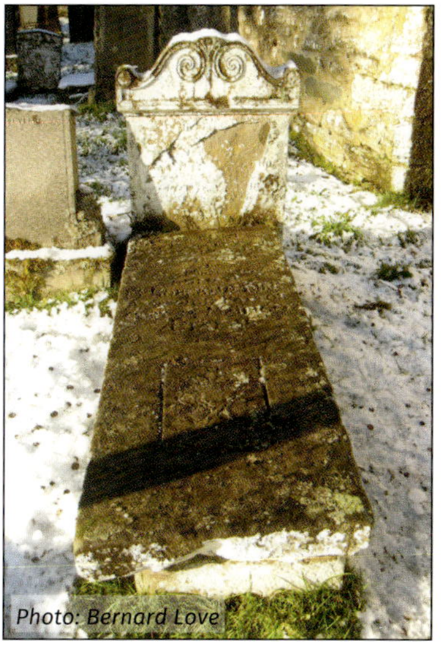

Kirk's Grave

An approximate translation is:

> *The former Minister of Aberfoyle,*
> *accurate promulgator and illuminator*
> *of the Irish Language [Gaelic],*
> *Robert Kirk, is buried here.*
> *Died* 14 *May* 1692, *aged* 48

It is interesting to speculate, in view of the date, 1793, that Patrick Graham organised centenary celebration for his eminent predecessor, Kirk, including tidying up his grave. It is known that Sir Walter Scott visited Graham in 1792, and the centenary might well have occasioned his interest in Kirk. However, this does not fit in with the date of Kirk's death stated by both Graham and by Scott.

In a happy phrase, Cunninghame Graham, in his *Notes on the District of Menteith* (1895) described Kirk as 'the astral vicar of Aberfoyle' which carries with it a prophetic hint of this. Nowadays Kirk might be described as an 'abductee', and 'the fairies' might be described as 'aliens'. Kirk's legendary experiences on the 'Fairy Hill' were, perhaps, 'close encounters' with a world we do not yet understand. Indeed, there are curious resemblances between the phenomena described by Kirk and the experiences of 'abductees'.

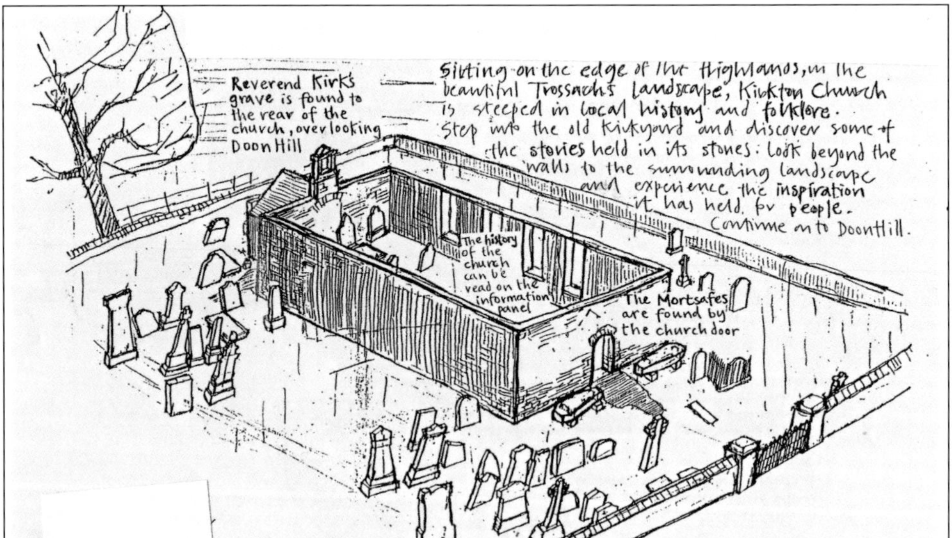

Image: Stirling Council

Kirkton: Plans for the Old Kirk

In *Horizon* (BBC2 28 November 1994) Professor Michael Persinger, a neurobiologist from the Laurentian University in Ontario, described experiments which he had carried out to stimulate hallucinations in the temporal lobes of volunteers with computer programmes which imitated the brain.

> "The experiences which are generated experimentally are primarily the fragments of abduction-type experiences and mystical-type experiences, and even the beginnings of some kinds of psychical or near-death experiences: pleasant vibrations, feelings of being light, leaving the body, perhaps a sense of a presence, also sensations that involve visual experiences – the feeling that it's a dream but it's more intense than a dream – very often the feelings that alter reality, feeling that the self is detached from the body. And sometimes sexual arousal occurs, which is a very important feature, because we find that many of these patterns are very much like the incubi and succubi reports of previous centuries, where people felt a sexual arousal at the time when the entity was visiting them."
>
> [Michael Persinger quoted in a transcript of *Horizon*]

This is very reminiscent of Kirk's *Secret Commonwealth*, in which detachment from reality, out-of-body experiences and succubi, for example, are frequent themes. Persinger went on to suggest that the kind of energy-release required to bring about these experiences might be explained by earth movements or earthquakes. Aberfoyle and Doon Hill are, of course, situated on the Highland Boundary Fault. Unfortunately, earthquakes at Comrie, situated on the same fault and undoubtedly the place most associated with earthquakes in Scotland, were not recorded until 1789. However, there was an earthquake in England in September 1692. Perhaps such earth movements might have taken place along the Highland Boundary Fault when Robert Kirk was 'taken'. Thus, Kirk's experiences can be seen as phenomena which continue to recur, which scientists are still seeking to explain, rather than something simply made up.

For his part, Cunninghame Graham was sceptical. In *Notes on the District of Menteith* he opined that Kirk's fairies were folk-memories of the Picts, 'with all due deference to Andrew Lang, to the Rev Mr. Kirk, and to the members of the Psychical Research Society.' His introduction to the Eneas Mackay reprint of Lang's edition of *The Secret Commonwealth* managed to enthuse about the book without commitment to it.

An intriguing aspect of Kirk's interest in fairies is the number of famous men it brought him into contact with, of whom **Robert Boyle** is the best known. Recent studies by Michael Hunter, Professor of History at Birkbeck College, the University of London have drawn more attention to Robert Boyle's interest in the paranormal. That such an eminently respectable scientist, who was one of the first to identify hydrogen, and whose 'law' is still one of the foundations of modern science, should be interested in the occult might be considered as shocking as an interest in fairies on the part of a minister of religion, but only with hindsight.

Hunter has shown that Boyle was a hypochondriac who used quack potions, and experimented with magic. As has long been known he was a secret alchemist, but it is now seen more clearly that he was also a dabbler in the occult; yet Boyle was also an extremely pious man who spent much of his fortune in making the Bible accessible. These interests make the connection between Robert Boyle and Robert Kirk, the Fairy Minister of Aberfoyle, a striking one. Boyle's involvement with Kirk, both of whom were seventh sons, comprehended both the religious and the supernatural. Boyle helped to finance Kirk's version of the Metrical Psalms, and Kirk's Gaelic Bible. For his part Kirk appended a letter addressed to Boyle from **George MacKenzie, Lord Tarbat** (1630–1714) to *The Secret Commonwealth*. The subject of the letter, written in response to an inquiry from Boyle, was 'Second Sight'. (Boyle's letter, displaying his interest in such matters, was suppressed by Birch, his first biographer). Perhaps because of Kirk's publication of it, Lord Tarbat's letter was widely circulated, and it was later quoted by Lord Reay, an early member of the Royal Society, in correspondence with **Samuel Pepys**. Pepys' interest in second sight was 'defence-related': he wondered whether it could provide 'naval intelligence'.

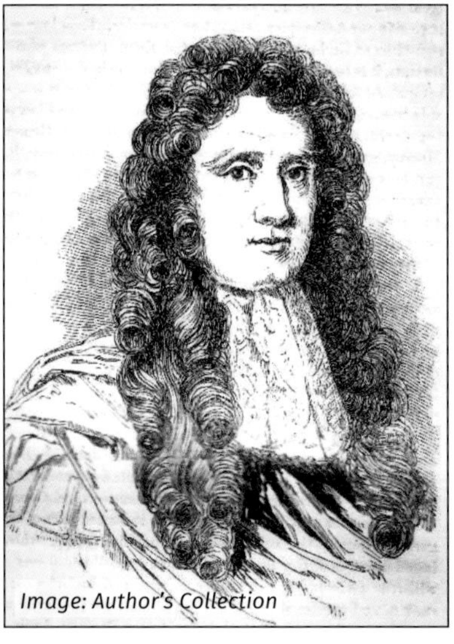

Lord Tarbat

An intriguing aspect of the letter is that Lord Tarbat states that he began to investigate second sight when he was 'confined to abide in the North of Scotland by the English usurpers.' He had joined the Earl of Glencairn's Rising against Cromwell of 1653–4, which began in Aberfoyle, and involved Graham of Duchray who was later to appear in the story of Robert Kirk in a significant capacity.

*

It may be difficult for us to appreciate it, but the Royal Society began by investigating both natural and supernatural phenomena. Boyle himself contributed papers at meetings dealing with both. It is part of Professor Hunter's argument that these interests in no way reflect on his qualities as a scientist or, for that matter, on his piety. Indeed, he reports Boyle's conscientiousness in resisting temptation in relation to the transmutation of metals, and his 'strong sense of anxiety about the power that alchemy might unleash.' Boyle's confidantes in these matters were **Gilbert Burnet** (1643–1715), an exiled Scot who became Bishop of Salisbury, and **Edward Stillingfleet** (1635–99), eventually Bishop of Worcester.

Notes which Kirk made when he was in London, supervising the publication of his Bible, illuminate this aspect of Boyle's life. He had an interview with Stillingfleet who said that 'occult phenomena like second sight entailed the danger of illicit contact with the Devil on the part of those who indulged in them and were therefore sinful.' Stillingfleet's wife, Elizabeth, uninhibited by her husband's views, expressed a wish to know more and it was for her that Kirk wrote the curious *The secret commonwealth, or, An essay on the nature and actions of the subterranean (and for the most part) invisible people heretofore going under the name of faunes and fairies, or the lyke, among the low country Scots, as they are described by those who have the second sight* (1691), in the form of a letter; a work later published in several different versions.

*

'Second sight' interested both statesmen and scientists in the seventeenth and eighteenth centuries and it tempted Scotland's most famous visitor, **Samuel Johnson**, to investigate it. Kirk was the first significant Scottish source to describe 'second sight', but two of his fellow countrymen, **John Fraser** (d.1702) and **Martin Martin** (c.1660–1719), also described instances of it, and the idea that 'second sight' was associated with the Western Isles rather than with, say, Perthshire, has become fixed in the public mind.

Daniel Defoe mentioned 'second sight' in *A tour thro' the whole island of Great Britain*, first published in three volumes between 1724 and 1727:

> "Mr Martin…gives an account of that called the Second Sight which he says is a representation by way of vision of something years to come, and makes such a strong impression upon the seers that they cannot see or think of anything else while the vision lasts, and they appear cheerful or otherwise according to the nature of the object represented. They use no previous means to attain it, and, to most of them, it is very troublesome. The instances of the truth of this Second Sight as it is called are so many and so frequent that it can scarcely be disputed it is certainly a strange illusion, but I shall not venture to give my opinion about it only observing with others that this faculty decays in proportion as Christianity increases among them, and as they improve in knowledge. Some of the people to whom those visions have been frequent have learned by experience, as I was told, to determine the time when the things represented shall come to pass. The Rev Mr John Fraser, a late Dean of the Isles, has written a small treatise upon this subject called *Deuteranopia*."

Interest in Kirk was revived early in the nineteenth century by **Walter Scott**, abetted by one of Kirk's successors, Rev. Patrick Graham. It was at this point that the legend of Kirk's death made its appearance. It has bedevilled Kirk's reputation ever since.

As a piece of folklore, the story is an appealing one. Briefly, it tells how Kirk was spirited away by the fairies while walking on a hill near the manse. He later appeared to a relation whom he told to persuade the local laird to attend the baptism of his (Kirk's) posthumous child, and, when he (Kirk) appeared, to throw a dagger above his head whereupon Kirk would be released from fairyland. Kirk appeared, but 'by some unaccountable fatality' the dagger was not thrown. Thus, Kirk is still captive in fairyland. Stewart Sanderson, Kirk's best-informed modern commentator, characterised it as 'apt, but faintly ludicrous'. Some folklorists have been anxious to espouse it, as if it gave authority to *The Secret Commonwealth*, rather than, perhaps, distracting attention from the scholarly reputation of the minister who wrote the book.

Whether it is true in any of its particulars, or not, the legend of Kirk's death has taken on a life of its own. It is frequently all that is known about Kirk, yet on examination the tale is rarely accurately told. The legend is interesting because it is of comparatively recent origin, it is unusually complex, involving many different folk elements, and it is continuing to evolve.

The story seems to have originated with **Patrick Graham** (1750–1832). It first appeared in the 1812 edition of *Sketches of Perthshire* (*see above*). Scott, in *Rob Roy* (1817), and subsequent authorities including Chambers' *Domestic Annals*, Andrew Lang, Evans Wenz, Lewis Spence, and Katharine Briggs seem to have relied on it. What is interesting about this is that the story did not appear in the first edition of Graham's book, although the learned minister did discourse on various other local superstitions in the 1806 edition. For example, a story about the fairy hill situated north of Loch Chon appears in the first edition. This is sometimes attributed to Kirk's contemporary **Martin Martin**, but Graham is the source of it. Graham originally produced the notes on which the guide book was based in 1792 for a visit which was made to the district by the famous artist **Joseph Farington**. He was collaborating with **John Knox** in producing what would have been one of the first illustrated books about Scottish scenery, but the project was abandoned when Knox died. The 1812 edition of *Sketches of Perthshire* was clearly produced in response to the enormous popular success of *The Lady of the Lake*, and contained a map illustrating the poem. In it Graham inserted the story of Kirk, which he prefaced with a reference to its resemblance to the Danish fairy story of the captivity in fairyland of Ethert Brand. This appears in what is called '*The Ballad of Alice Brand*' in Canto IV of *The Lady of the Lake*. Scott freely acknowledged that it was from Graham that he obtained many of the local superstitions which he incorporated in his world-famous poem. In *Sketches* Graham returned the compliment.

Maclean suggests that Graham made this story up, and it does contain several inconsistencies. As was pointed out by Maclean, Graham, unaccountably, got Kirk's date of birth, and thus his age, wrong. Maclean quotes the beginning of the inscription on Kirk's gravestone. On the gravestone at present in the old kirkyard, which was last refurbished between 1880 and 1904 during the incumbency of Rev William Taylor, the date of Kirk's death and his age are given. It seems unlikely that the gravestone was so illegible in

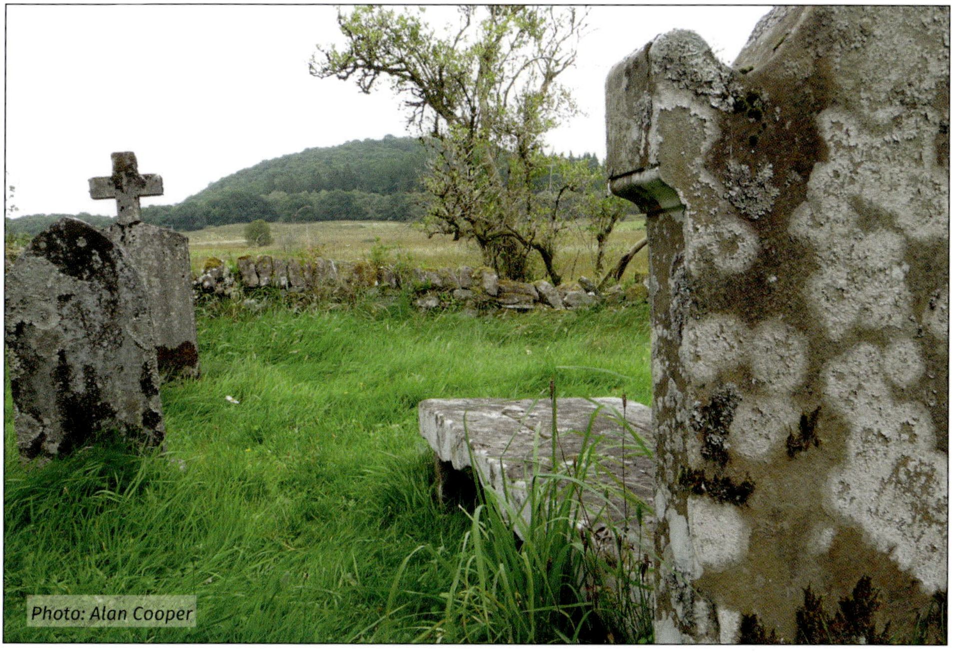

Doon Hill from Kirk's Grave

Graham's time that he couldn't read it, so why he got this wrong – and confused Scott – is inexplicable. Graham may also have made another important mistake. He stated that Kirk was walking "upon a little eminence to the west of the present manse which is still reckoned a Dun Shie . . ." The 'Doon Hill' which is popularly supposed locally to be the hill on which Kirk was taken is east of the manse, not west of it. Kirkton Hill is west of the manse. It can be added that another hill, still called the Fairy Knowe, and an altogether more likely spot than either, is south of the manse. These two errors on Graham's part may simply be careless mistakes. Furthermore, Graham of Duchray, who features in the story of Kirk, was over ninety years of age when Kirk's child was baptised. However, it is probably his son, Thomas Graham, who is referred to. Indeed, it is not surprising that a ninety-year-old failed to throw the dagger above Kirk's head. That this should not have been pointed out by Graham can be characterised as slipshod, but this omission, together with the errors, suggest that he did not take the story very seriously.

Scott took his information about Kirk from Graham and compounded his mistakes in *Rob Roy* (1819). An illustration of the way in which things get distorted is that in early editions of *Rob Roy* the note about Kirk states that he appeared to a 'medical' relation of himself and of Graham of Duchray. Graham's version was a 'mutual' relation, altogether more understandable. However, it is Scott's misprint which has most often survived in the telling of the tale.

Lewis Spence analysed Graham's narrative, and drew attention to the similarities which there are between it and fairy stories about mothers-in-milk being taken by the fairies, and other folk tales surrounding childbirth. Kirk's wife was pregnant when he died, and Spence suggests that it is understandable that, in these circumstances, some of these folk-beliefs were transferred to him. Spence's conclusion is that the story of Kirk's death contains a number of elements from a variety of folk tales. It is not difficult to see how Kirk's known interest in 'fairies' might have led local people to surround his death with various stories of this sort. Of these, one, not relayed by Graham, attaches to Kirk's grave. One might suppose that if Kirk was kidnapped by the fairies, they would have left a stock, indistinguishable from Kirk himself, and that this 'body' would have been buried. However, it is sometimes said (e.g. as reported by Evans Wenz) that his coffin was filled with stones which would have been quite unnecessary. With an empty sepulchre, and Kirk's later re-appearance at the baptism, the story begins to bear an uncomfortable resemblance to the Resurrection. This addition to the story can safely be dismissed as a fabrication.

In her authoritative *Dictionary of British Folk Tales* (1971) **Katharine Briggs** rather oddly chose to use Andrew Lang's account of Kirk's death. Lang's introduction to *The Secret Commonwealth* puts Kirk in context, referring, for example, to such topics as psychical research and to folk tales from elsewhere in the world, but his telling of the tale of Kirk's death is very much second hand. Katharine Briggs appended her own contribution to Kirk's legend. She told Stewart Sanderson, in a private communication, that she met a young woman in Methven in 1943 who was expecting a baby:

> "She...was anxious to get back to the Manse before it was born, for the local tradition was that, if a baby was born in the manse and christened there, Kirk could be freed from fairyland if a dirk was thrust into the seat of his chair..."
>
> *Penguin Dictionary of Fairies*

The dislike of fairies for iron is said, according to one theory, to arise from the fact that fairies were the pre-iron age inhabitants of the country. Katharine Briggs told Sanderson that she believed that this story was only 'a whimsical belief on her part'. In other words, it was simply a significant example of the longevity of the legend. As a result of an inquiry from an American correspondent I recently investigated this story locally. Two features of it are inaccurate: the Manse was not let during the War, it was occupied by the Minister and his family; nor was there a chair there supposed to have been Kirk's. It seems likely that the young woman concerned was the wife of an officer billeted in Manse Road. Her baby was born in Aberfoyle in 1941, and was baptised 'Robert'.

One of the more recent additions to the legend is an encounter with Robert Kirk reported by R. J. Stewart in *Earthlight*. This took place in 1982, and it is described by Stewart in terms which permit the reader to interpret it as a personal spiritual experience.

Stewart is a serious student of such phenomena who has written several books, and is well-regarded in his field. He describes visiting Doon Hill where he found himself 'communing with someone' who 'was a short man, fairly plump, who declared himself to be Robert Kirk'. An unkind explanation would be that there were two eccentrics on the hill that day. Stewart goes on to describe how Kirk invited him to join him in fairy land, and how he came to his senses when he heard a car horn. In the book he describes his experience in a way which allows that he may simply have fallen asleep. He subsequently produced a modern edition of *The Secret Commonwealth*. Strikingly, he did not mention his own experience of Kirk in that book.

KIRK'S BIBLE

It might seem surprising, since the most famous version of the Bible in English bears the name of a Scottish King and dates from 1611, that, for most of the seventeenth century, there was no printed version in the Scottish vernacular; that is, there was no attempt to produce a printed version in the Scots Tongue, and no printed version accessible to Gaelic speakers. This latter was partly a product of the intolerant view that Gaelic speakers were difficult enough without being given access to the Bible.

*

It was while he was in Balquhidder which was then entirely Gaelic speaking that the scholarly Kirk worked on a Gaelic version of fifty metrical psalms *Psalma Dhaibhidh an meadrachd*, 221 copies of which were published in 1684. He had learned that the synod of Argyll intended to publish a rival version, and he resorted to curious expedients to keep himself awake while working night and day to forestall them. This work was printed in Irish characters, and Episcopalian in origin, so it did not please everyone; although it was, for about ten years, the only version of the psalms in Gaelic available, after which another, more complete version began to supersede it. However, it was because of this work that Kirk became involved with the revision of a printed version in Gaelic of the *Charteris Catechism* (1688), the production and distribution of which was financed by **Robert Boyle** (1627–91). It may be noted here that Kirk produced a small vocabulary to be used with the Bible, in effect a forerunner of future Gaelic Dictionaries.

Boyle was the Irish philosopher and scientist who enunciated several principles on which modern science is based, of which his "law" that, at a constant temperature the volume of a gas is inversely proportional to the pressure, is the best known. He was a director of the East India Company and used his wealth to further the distribution of the Bible, getting it translated, for example into Turkish. Unsurprisingly he was concerned to obtain an Irish version, and in 1685 a translation of both the Old Testament [by Bedell], and the New Testament [by O'Donnell] – but not the Apocrypha because Boyle objected – was printed in a new Irish type which Boyle paid for.

Rev. James Kirkwood (1650[?]–1708), a Scot ministering to a flock in Bedfordshire, who had been deprived of his living in Scotland because, unlike Kirk, he had refused to take the 'Test', urged Boyle to distribute this Bible [The Bedell Bible] in the Highlands, and obtained 221 copies, supposedly enough to provide one Bible for each Parish. Kirk, and his lawyer-relative Colin Campbell of Carwhin, agent to the Earl of Breadalbane, took responsibility for its distribution in the Highlands. Kirk also produced a small vocabulary of 464 difficult words, which foreshadowed future Gaelic dictionaries; this was later revised and republished in 1702 by the Welsh scholar **Edward Lhuyd** (*d.* 1709).

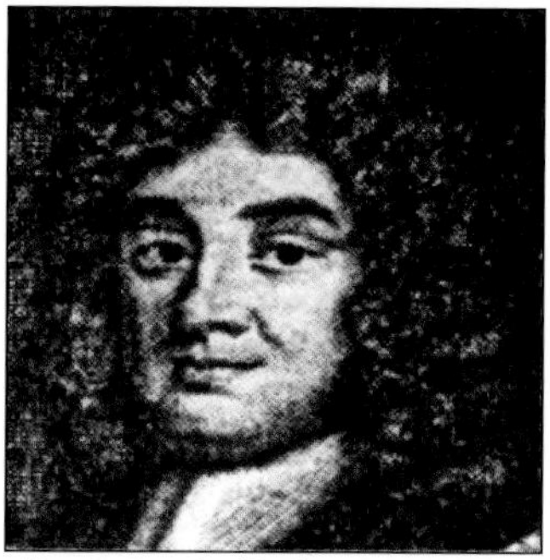

[Source Not Identified]

Edward Stillingfleet

The Bibles were inscribed by Kirk with a certificate paying tribute to Boyle.

Kirk regarded the number of Bibles available as ridiculous, partly because many of them were 'alienated to private use'. The Irish characters were unfamiliar to the Highlanders, and Kirk proposed that more copies should be made available, transliterated into Roman characters. Boyle agreed to contribute to the cost. Kirk undertook this huge task himself in 1688–89. This was a greatly troubled time, following the accession of William and Mary of Orange. Nevertheless, the intrepid Minister of Aberfoyle went to London for eight months to supervise the printing of what came to be known as Kirk's Bible, completed by April 1690. While in London, Kirk, who had a keen interest in fairy superstitions, met **Bishop Edward Stillingfleet** and his wife, Elizabeth. The bishop was a seventh son, and the couple, who were themselves to have seven sons, were intrigued by what this might imply. They asked Kirk for further information. It was in response that he wrote *The Secret Commonwealth* (*see following section*).

Kirkwood, who can be regarded as one of the founders of Scottish libraries because he suggested the establishment of a 'bibliotheck' in every Parish, continued the task of distributing the bibles after Kirk's death.

THE SECRET COMMONWEALTH

Pious ministers have long been properly interested in the beliefs of their parishioners, and in recording them. Kirk's *Secret Commonwealth* is one of the earliest surviving documents of this sort. It is thus a precursor of the many collections of folk tales of the Highlands and Islands which have been made since. Yet Kirk's interest in the spiritual – both in what might be perceived as evil spirits and in the Christian religion – is, perhaps, difficult for us to comprehend nowadays. He has always interested folklorists; and successive generations of them have descended on Aberfoyle to visit his grave. It is when he seems to be an apostle of the occult, asserting that there is evidence for 'second sight', and for the existence of an alternative society of 'subterraneans' that difficulties arise. His pious successors have sometimes asserted that such beliefs are best dismissed.

*

In his introduction to *The Secret Commonwealth* Cunninghame Graham points out that the citizens of Aberfoyle in his day adhered strongly to their Presbyterian faith:

> "I remember when in the Inn (it was not in those days called an Hotel) there hung an almanac in the entrance hall, containing the announcement, '12th of August. Grouse shooting opens. Episcopacy abolished.'"

He goes on to remind us that, despite all the religious upheaval which took place during the seventeenth century, Kirk was, so far as he was permitted to be, an Episcopalian. Indeed, Graham goes on to surmise, with his tongue in his cheek, that Kirk was a changeling from birth, a spy sent by the fairies to make their ways manifest. Kirk says that one reason for compiling his treatise was 'to suppress the impudent and growing atheism of our age', although this was a common way of dedicating books. However, the book is prefaced by quotations from the Bible.

On the one hand it seems decidedly odd, not to say dangerous, that a Minister should have any truck with fairies at that time; on the other hand, one can imagine that a Minister genuinely interested in the spiritual welfare of his flock might wish to develop an understanding of the primitive beliefs which were as firmly held by country folk in the seventeenth century as Christian beliefs. As Kirk puts it:

> "How much is written of pigmies, fairies, nymphs, syrens and apparitions which, though not the tenth part true, could not spring of nothing."

Robert Kirk *The Secret Commonwealth* 1691

The title of Kirk's book is comprehensive, one version being as follows:

> *Secret Commonwealth: or an Essay on the Nature and Actions of the Subterranean (and for the most part) Invisible People heretofore going under the names of Fauns and Fairies, or the like, among the Low Country Scots as described by those who have second sight.*

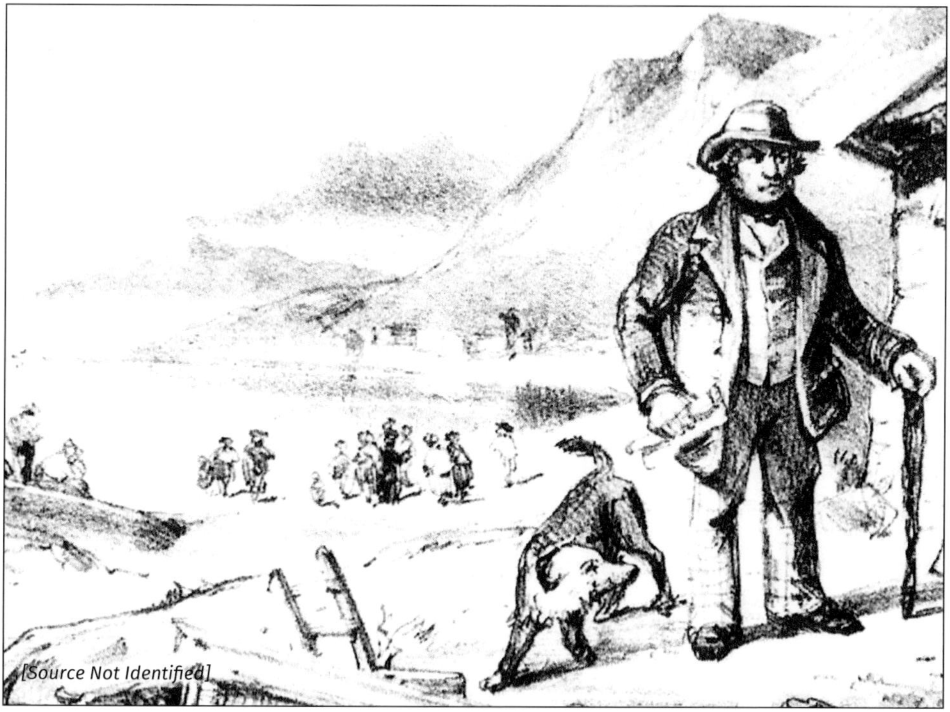

[Source Not Identified]

How Fairies Might Look

In it Kirk gives a comprehensive account of the lives of various kinds of fairies including details of their social organisation, their habits, their dwelling places, what they ate, their crafts, their faults 'envy, spite, hypocrisy, lying and dissimulation', and, even, their sex lives:

> "In our Highlands there be many fair Ladies of this aerial order which do often tryst with lascivious young men in the quality of succubi, or lightsome paramours and strumpets."

The whole book is very matter of fact, a scientific work of much merit. Sanderson points out that there are some inconsistencies which are not worked out, for example between fairies which live in groups and fairies of individual habits, but it is an impressive and detailed treatise with very few inconsistencies once the reader accepts the proposition that there are fairies. J. M. Barrie and other purveyors of whimsy have done much to damage the image of fairies which, if you read Kirk's book, seem much more like an alternative society to our own. Some seem likeable, others more menacing, and they are by no means all the insubstantial "little people" of popular imagination. Kirk believed that they wore clothes like those of the country where they lived.

Kirk takes a scientific line, reporting the visits he has undertaken to verify his information. He reports that when he was in Balquhidder he went to visit a woman of forty years of age possessed by fairies, to examine her and verify her story (being careful to take a colleague with him). Cunninghame Graham comments wittily on how wise this was:

> "This certainly showed his discretion, a quality rarely conspicuous among the clergy, who are too prone at times to examine ladies, even less than forty years of age, without a witness of their own cloth to testify that their intentions were innocuous."

As a seventh son, Kirk had the gift of healing and the gift of second sight which is supposed to be conferred on seventh sons. He explains, at some length, that these gifts must be developed. Second sight enabled Kirk to see the Good People, fairies always being referred to by circumlocutions, as 'a rapture, transport, and a sort of death'. As an illustration of the powers exercised by seers Kirk points out that 'the minor sort of seers prognosticate many future events from the shoulder bone of a sheep, on which a knife never came… by examining the bone they will tell of whoredom to be committed in the owner's house, what money the master of the sheep had…' He also relates the story of a yeoman from Killin who went to an ale house where a seer was sitting at a table. When the yeoman entered the seer got up to leave. When he was asked why he was in such a hurry, he said the yeoman would be dead within two days. This so incensed the yeoman that he stabbed the seer, and was executed for murder within two days, thus fulfilling the seer's prediction. Modern readers might detect a moral tale drawing attention to the evils of drink, rather than a particularly convincing example of a seer's powers, but Kirk illustrates his book with many such stories which make *The Secret Commonwealth* a lively piece of work. In view of the way in which his life came to an end, what Kirk has to say about fairy hills and about doppelgangers is of interest. It has been pointed out by more than one observer that Doon Hill, the fairy hill above Aberfoyle, resembles an ancient hill fort, having the appearance of an artificial mound rather than a natural hill. Indeed, it is probable that its name is derived from 'dun', the word used in Gaelic for 'a fortified mound' of this type. This hypothesis has never been tested by archaeologists, but the resemblance may well have been sufficient to persuade local people that the hill was occupied by the prehistoric inhabitants of the district. From this supposition it is then a short step to the fairies because one explanation for them is that they constitute a folk memory of earlier pagan inhabitants. Kirk states that there are many places called fairy hills, which the mountain people think it impious to strip or uncover by taking earth or wood from them, superstitiously believing that the souls of their predecessors dwell there. Kirk describes how doppelgangers ('the shape of the same man in two places that is a super-terranean and a sub-terranean inhabitant perfectly resembling one another in all points') are clearly seen by men of second sight at funerals. 'They call this reflex man a Co-Walker, every way like the man, as a twin-brother and companion, haunting him as his shadow, oft seen and known among men, both before and after the original is dead.'

A good precis of *The Secret Commonwealth* is provided by **Sir Walter Scott** in his *Letters on Demonology and Witchcraft.* (1830)

> "In this discourse, the author, 'with undoubting mind', describes the fairy race as a sort of astral spirits, of a kind betwixt humanity and angels – says that they have children, nurses, marriages, deaths, and burials, like mortals in appearance; that in some respect they represent mortal men, and that individual apparitions, or Double-men, are found among them, corresponding with mortals existing on earth. Mr. Kirk accuses them of stealing the milk from cows, and of carrying away what is more material, the women in pregnancy, and new-born children from their nurses. The remedy is easy in both cases. The milk cannot be stolen, if the mouth of the calf, before he is permitted to suck, be rubbed with a certain balsam, very easily come by; and the woman in travail is safe, if a piece of cold iron is put in the bed. Mr Kirk accounts for this, by informing us, that the great northern mines of iron, lying adjacent to the place of eternal punishment, have a savour odious to these 'fascinating creatures'. They have, says the reverend author, what one would not expect, many light toyish books, (novels and plays, doubtless) others on Rosicrucian subjects, and of an abstruse mystical character; but they have no Bibles or works of devotion. The essayist fails not to mention the elf-arrowheads, which have something of the subtlety of thunderbolts, and can mortally wound the vital parts, without breaking the skin. These wounds, he says, he has himself observed in beasts, and felt the fatal lacerations which he could not see."

The Secret Commonwealth is a book which anyone seriously interested in fairies is recommended to read.

FAIRIES FROM ABERFOYLE AND ELSEWHERE

The following alphabetical list provides a guide to the fairies dealt with by Kirk in *The Secret Commonwealth*, and to other fairies likely to be encountered in the district. It is certainly incomplete, but it has been compiled with reference to E.C.Brewer (1810–97) *Dictionary of Phrase and Fable* (1978), and Katharine Briggs *A Dictionary of Fairies* (1976), as well as from Kirk, and other sources:

Apparition A ghost; anything shocking or startling which appears.

Banshee Irish (or Highland Scottish) domestic spirit; in Gaelic Bean-sith, a woman fairy; connected with the death of women in childbirth.

Bocan Hobgoblin, or spirit. In Menteith the uruisks at one time resided at Goblin Knowe, Cnoc nan Bocan; an outlier of Ben Lomond, above Rowchoish, is Creag a' Bhocain.

Boggart Local hobgoblin or spirit (Scottish); a bad-tempered, or ill – natured Brownie.

Bogle A bugbear (Scottish); a bogie.

Brollachan *see* Fuath.

Brownie English/Scottish fairy varying a little in characteristics from place to place; most notably associated with the Borders

> *Defined by Scott as a familiar spirit 'believed in ancient times to supply the deficiencies of the ordinary labourer.' A moron compared with sprightlier beings like the fairies, the brownie is good-natured in nocturnal chores, ill-natured in occasional rough treatment of women. It is easily pleased and just as easily offended. Both Sir Walter Scott and his friend, James Hogg, display an almost sentimental attachment to the last of the Border lubber spirits, the Brownie of Bodesbeck. In the second volume of his novel, however, Hogg confesses 'This celebrated Brownie was no other than the noted Mr John Brown of Caldwell.'*
>
> Parsons *Witchcraft and Demonology in Scott's Fiction* 1964

Bug (Bugbear) Any imaginary thing that frightens a person.

Changeling *see* **Stock**.

Co-walker Kirk's name for a Double, or Doppelganger; a wraith.

Dobby Household sprite; word for a ghost in Yorkshire.

Droich Dwarf; possibly a metathesis of duergar (used by Cunninghame Graham in his introduction to *The Secret Commonwealth*).

Drow (Troll) Drows or Trows, according to Scott, are 'somewhat allied to the fairies, residing, like them, in the interior of green hills and caverns.' More frequently hostile to than friendly to man, these subterranean people are particularly dangerous at midnight. They are skilled metal workers.

Dryad (Hamadryad) Wood-nymph (Classical); Cunninghame-Graham suggests that, in Menteith, local people 'replaced the nymphs and hamadryads by the fairies' [*At Dalmary* (short story)].

Duergar Gotho-German dwarfs, dwelling in rocks and hills. The English fairy (or Gothic elf) whose prototype is to be sought chiefly in the bergelfen or duergar of the Scandinavians may in turn go back to the diminutive Lapps, Finns, and Letts.

> *Being excellent metallurgists and meteorologists, these dwarfish refugees worked in underground hideouts and, gaining a supernatural reputation, were associated, or confounded, with, German kobolds, English goblins, and Scottish bogles, as also with the vivacious fairy kind.*
>
> Parsons *Witchcraft and Demonology in Scott's Fiction* 1964

Dwarf A diminutive being (natural or supernatural).

Each Uisge The water-horse; lives in both sea lochs and fresh water lochs.

Elf In Scandinavia fairies of diminutive size; fond of practical jokes. Anglo-Saxon word for spirits of any sort. Kirk states that they used not to exceed an ell in height. Scott had the following comment:

> *Sprites of the coarser sort, more laborious vocation and more malignant temper and, in all respects, less propitious to humanity than the Fairies*
>
> Sir Walter Scott *Letters on Witchcraft and Demonology* 1828

Fairy (Faerie) A supernatural being, fond of pranks, but generally friendly; in Gaelic Duine-sith (also Daoine Sidhe); a fairy person, or fairy folk, people of peace:

> *Fairies, if not positively malevolent, are capricious, and easily offended. They are, like other proprietors of the forest, peculiarly jealous of their rights of vert and venison. This jealousy was also an attribute of the northern Duergar, or dwarfs; to many of whose distinctions the fairies seem to have succeeded, if, indeed, they are not the same class of beings.*
>
> Walter Scott *The Lady of the Lake* (1810)

Fay Same as **fairy**; Fée in French and German.

Faun Rural god with the horns and legs of a goat (Classical) – comparable with uruisks; Kirk defines Fauns as a rank of Demon betwixt Angels and Men.

Fuath Collective term for independent spirits, or solitary fairies (as opposed to Trooping Fairies), generally malignant, properly associated with water; includes uruisks.

Glaistig A woman fairy; half-woman, half-goat; combines most fairy characteristics being rather like a Brownie, fond of children, old people and the feeble-minded, but also misleads travellers.

Gnome The guardian of mines and quarries (Germanic).

Goblin (Hobgoblin) A phantom spirit.

The deep-voiced, square-built, long armed Rob Roy seems to Frank Osbaldistone ferocious, cunning and unearthly like 'the old Picts who ravaged Northumberland, a sort of half-goblin, half-human being' in Scott's novel.

Good Folk The Brownies, or house spirits.

Gruagach A damsel; a bridesmaid; a supposed household goddess; a brownie.

Habitrot The spinning-wheel fairy.

Hag A female fury.

Hobgoblin 'Hob' is 'Robin', thought to soften the word 'goblin'.

Household Spirits

England Robin Goodfellow
France Esprit Follet
Germany Kobold
Scotland Brownie or Uruisg
Wales Tylwyth Teg

Ignis Fatuus A phosphorescent light which hovers over marshy ground, supposedly due to the spontaneous combustion of gasses; called a jack-a-lantern or will o' the wisp.

Imp Puny demon, or spirit of mischief.

Jack-a-Lantern A bog, or marsh spirit which delights to mislead.

Kelpie Imaginary spirit of the waters generally in the form of a horse; malignant towards human beings, luring them into the water where they drowned. Loch Chon and Loch Venachar, in the Trossachs, have kelpies; the kelpie, associated with running water, is sometimes distinguished from the Each Uisge, the water-horse, associated with lochs and sea-lochs

Ko**bold** A German household goblin; also frequents mines.

Leannain Sith Familiar spirits.

Luspardan Kind of fairy, referred to by Kirk; dwarf or sprite.

Naiad (Naiades) Water-nymph (Classical); Akenside and Turner saw Scottish waterfalls as likely haunts for them.

Pegths, or **Pechs** Traditional lowland name for fairies; identified as a folk-memory of the Picts.

Satyr Rural god, half-goat and half-man (Classical).

Seer In connection with folklore, a person gifted with second sight; Kirk points out that they are usually men, 'females being seldom so qualified'.

Sitheach A fairy.

Siths People at rest, or at peace; a circumlocution for fairies.

Sithean Fairy, fairies.
Sith Bruach: a fairy hill
Sidheag Biorach: the pointed fairy knoll, is situated above Loch Chon
Ben an-t-sithein: the fairy ben, above Loch Lubnaig
Cnoc nan Sidheag: the fairy knoll, in Glenfinglas

> *About a mile beyond the source of the Forth, above Lochon, there is a place called Coir-shi'an, or the Cove of the Men of Peace, which is still supposed to be a favourite place of their residence. In the neighbourhood, are to be seen many round, conical eminences; particularly one, near the head of the lake; by the skirts of which, many are still afraid to pass after sun-set. It is believed that if, on Hallow-eve, any person alone, goes round one of these hills nine times, towards the left hand (sinistrorsum), a door shall open, by which he shall be admitted into their subterraneous abodes.*

Patrick Graham *Sketches of Perthshire* 1806

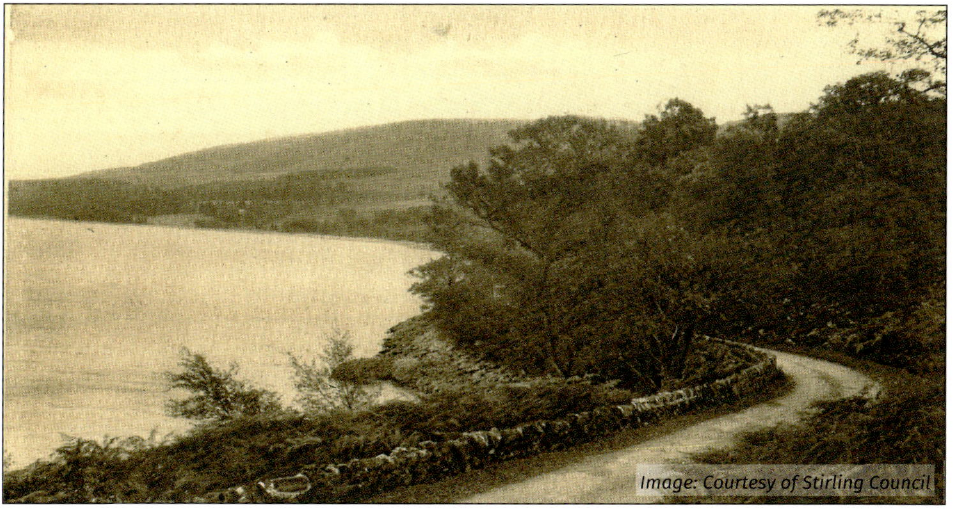

Loch Venachar: The Wood of Lamentation

Sluagh [Sleag] Maith The Good People; the host of the dead.

Stic Gaelic equivalent of Puck.

Stock Changeling substituted by the fairies when they stole a baby; a substitute; explains how Kirk, who was supposed to be imprisoned by the fairies, could be buried in the churchyard.

Subterraneans Kirk's word for the fairies who lived underground, possibly the spirits of the departed; a different explanation is that they were a folk memory of the Picts, some of whom lived in subterranean dwellings.

Succubus A demon in female form, supposed to have carnal intercourse with men in their sleep [OED]. In *Glenfinlas* Scott describes how the dale got its reputation as the 'Glen of the Green Women'. Kirk describes the sex life of fairies suggesting that succubi were common.

Tacharan Sprite; ghost

Troll A hill-spirit (Norwegian); dislikes noise (*see* Drow).

Trooping Fairies Fairies who moved from place to place, and lived together, as distinct from Solitary Fairies like uruisks, etc.

Uruisk or **Uruisg** Highland (domestic) spirit; *see* Brownie; very lucky to have about the house; sometimes thought to be half-human half-goat; solitary in nature, frequently haunting waterfalls, but uruisks were supposed to meet together at times; easily insulted and quick to take offence.

> *Coire nan Uruisgean: Ben Venue is rendered venerable in the superstition of the natives, by the celebrated Coire nan Uruisgean, the cove or recess of goblins, situated on the northern side of the mountain, overhanging the lake in gloomy grandeur. The Uruisks were a sort of lubberly supernaturals, who, like the Brownies of England, could be gained over by kind attentions, to perform the drudgery of the farm; and it was believed that many families in the Highlands had one of their order attached to it. They were supposed to be dispersed over the Highlands, each with his own wild recess; but the solemn stated meetings of the order were regularly held in this cave of Ben Venue. The current superstition, no doubt, alludes to some circumstance in the ancient history of this country: perhaps it may have taken its rise, like the superstition of the Daone Shie, or Men of Peace, from the abolition and proscription of the Druidical order, under the Fingallian dynasty.*
>
> Patrick Graham *Sketches of Perthshire* 1806

Will o' the Wisp Spirit of the bogs; misleads benighted travellers.

Wight Wraith-like creature.

Wraith Ghost of a person about to die or just dead; it was Kirk's wraith which was said to have appeared at the baptism of his daughter.

THE LITERARY INFLUENCE OF ROBERT KIRK

Kirk's *The Secret Commonwealth* is widely quoted today in learned treatises about folklore, but it also provides, as a book, a focal point in the literary history of the District. One of Kirk's successors as Minister of Aberfoyle, Patrick Graham (1750–1835), was, in his own right, a distinguished author who wrote about both the topography and the fairy lore of the district. Sir Walter Scott (1771–1832), who relied on Graham for his local knowledge, used the folk history and the history of the district in various ways. Scott's admirers included Charles Nodier (1780–1844), the French Romantic, writer of short stories and fairy tales; Hans Christian Andersen (1805–75), one of the world's greatest fairy-storytellers; and Jules Verne (1828–1905), founder of Science Fiction and exponent of the fantastic, all of whom visited, and were enchanted by the Trossachs. Andrew Lang (1844–1912), the prolific late Victorian writer, made his reputation as a man of letters, partly at least, because of his interest in folklore. This led him to edit *The Secret Commonwealth*, and to write his poem about Kirk. He connected Kirk's interest in the supernatural with Robert Louis Stevenson (1850–94). Later R. B. Cunninghame Graham (1852–1936), laird of Gartmore, situated at the foot, almost, of Kirk's fairy hill, followed Lang in introducing a further edition of the book. He too had a strong interest in the preternatural. Another writer with strong roots in the locality who often wrote about Kirk was Alasdair Alpin MacGregor (1889–1970).

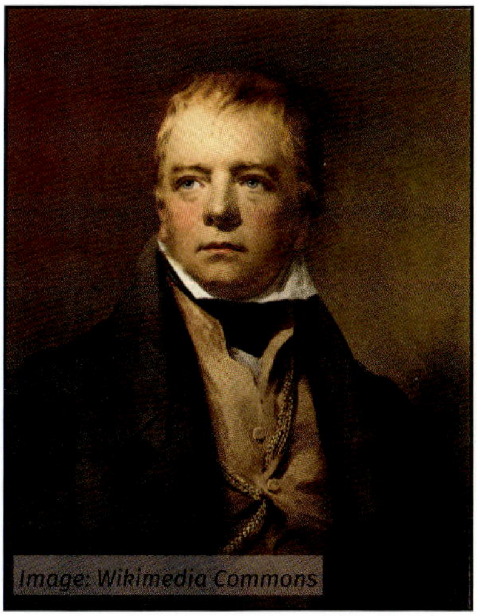

Sir Walter Scott

*

Patrick Graham was Minister of the Parish from 1787 to 1835. He was a literary scholar who was well known beyond the district, and took a prominent part in the controversy about the authenticity of MacPherson's *Ossian*. There might be some dispute about who 'discovered' the Trossachs, but Graham must take some credit. His description of the Trossachs in *Sketches of Perthshire* influenced both the Wordsworths and Scott. Graham included a substantial section in his guide book about the superstitions of the district thus perpetuating, a hundred years after Kirk's death, interest in the subject. Scott, who visited Graham frequently, clearly relied on him to provide local colour for both *The Lady of the Lake* and *Rob Roy*. Scott 'killed' Graham in a footnote to Rob Roy. When acknowledging his debt to him Scott stated that 'the respectable clergyman alluded to has been dead for some years.' Graham's urbanity is illustrated by this witty letter to Scott, which mentions Kirk, written when he was nearly eighty years old:

> Manse of Aberfoyle 31 December 1829
> From the Rev Patrick Graham
>
> Dear Sir Walter
> The second volume of the new edition of Rob Roy reached this remote spot two days ago; and afforded a renewal of the pleasure which its first perusal excited, enhanced as it was by intimate acquaintance with the localities and individual characters so strikingly portrayed in it, till in a note on p 203 I lighted on the startling information that I have been dead some years. Though till now unconscious of this very material change in the scene and mode of my existence, I am far from questioning a fact stated on such high authority. As is often the case my consciousness and my deference to testimony stand strangely opposed to each other. I scarcely know whether I am alive or dead, but the weight of evidence in favour of my death seems on the whole to preponderate, and to that I am bound, as a sound reasoner, to submit implicitly. Perhaps, indeed, like a well-known predecessor of my own, I have been only carried off by the Daoine Shie, in which case the unearthly being who now addresses you may be no more than a Fairy Changeling, left for a time to occupy the place of the departed Minister of Aberfoyle. At any rate the time and the manner in which the intelligence reached me have given me the singular gratification of enjoying my own posthumous fame. To be praised by the author of Rob Roy might well make any man proud, but to receive and read that praise so long after my death is what I believe no Mortal but myself would ever boast of. Still the pleasure this affords is attended with some inconvenience. My daughter, stunned by the discovery, has hurried home from Glasgow to ascertain the circumstances of her father's decease. My noble Patron is overwhelmed with letters from Celtic divines of every patronymic detailing their claims and offering their services to supply the vacancy. The Presbytery of the bounds, considering the time which has elapsed, have held a meeting pro re nata, with a view to the exercise of their jus devolutum. And, worst of all, my old servant Duncan, who has been in his day a jack-of-all-trades , and does not scruple to borrow an hour now and then from his sleep or his work – as it may happen – to spell the pages of a diverting story, insists on receiving a complete suit of decent mourning for his dear and good master, for which demand he finds in the tale both reason and precedent After all I believe I must lay my death at your door; but as a dying man, and much more a dead man, is bound to forgive even the author of his death, I beg leave to assure you of the unabated respect and regard with which I am, or should rather say I was, dear Sir Walter, your sincere friend and warm admirer,
> *Pat Graham*

Scott apologised to Graham, who wrote to him again urging the novelist to leave the passage as it was "I am truly sorry that you have felt uneasiness about the mistake made in your beautiful novel *Rob Roy* in the mention of my name, to which, on many occasions, you have done so much honour… I must soon be entitled to the epithet which you have employed." Scott then made his apology public in a note in an edition of *The Legend of Montrose* which begins in the Trossachs:

> "It is with mingled pleasure and shame that I record the important error of having announced as deceased my learned acquaintance, the Rev. Dr Graham, Minister of Aberfoyle. I cannot now recollect the precise ground of my depriving my learned and excellent friend of his existence, unless like Mr Kirk, his predecessor in the parish, the excellent Doctor has made a short trip to Fairyland, with whose wonders he is so well acquainted. But however, I may have been misled, my regret is most sincere for having spread such a rumour; and no one can be more gratified than I that the report, however I may have been induced to give it credit and currency, is a false one, and that Dr Graham is still the living pastor of Aberfoyle, for the delight and instruction of his brother antiquaries."

However, Aberfoyle is principally associated with Scott's *Rob Roy*. It is interesting to note that Scott had already written *The Lady of the Lake* and provided notes elaborating on the folklore of the district to accompany the poem, and that he set some scenes from *Waverley*, published in 1814, in the district. In 1815 he edited an edition of *The Secret Commonwealth*, so he was fully steeped in the traditions of the locality when he came to write *Rob Roy*. This complex novel is about inheritance, family quarrels over a business enterprise involving embezzlement, and, of course, unrequited love. It is set at first in England, and involves a journey to Scotland which enables Scott to describe the Roman Wall near Carlisle, Glasgow, and the vicinity of Aberfoyle in his inimitable way. Frank Osbaldistone, an Englishman, is the narrator. He describes the party's first encounter with the Forth:

> "We found ourselves at length on the bank of a stream, which rather resembled one of my native English rivers than those I had hitherto seen in Scotland. It was narrow, deep, still, and silent, although the imperfect light as it gleamed on its placid waters, showed also that we were now among the lofty mountains which formed its cradle. "That's the Forth," said the Bailie with an air of reverence, which I have observed the Scots usually pay to their distinguished rivers. The Clyde, the Tweed, the Forth, the Spey, are usually named by those who dwell on their banks with a sort of respect and pride, and I have known duels occasioned by any word of disparagement. I cannot say I have the least quarrel with this sort of enthusiasm."

The next passage illustrates admirably the way in which Scott uses folklore as a literary device to create atmosphere. His description of the fairies is derived from Kirk:

> "The Forth, however, as far as the imperfect light permitted me to judge, seemed to merit the admiration of those who claimed an interest in the stream. A beautiful eminence of the most regular round shape, and clothed with copsewood of hazels, mountain-ash, and dwarf oak, intermixed with a few magnificent old trees, which rising above the underwood, exposed their forked and bared branches to the silver moonshine, seemed to protect the sources from which the river sprung. If I could trust the tale of my companion, which, while professing to disbelieve every word of it, he told under his breath, and with an air of something like intimidation, this hill, so regularly formed, so richly verdant, and garlanded with such a beautiful variety of ancient trees and thriving copsewood, was held by the neighbourhood to contain, within its unseen caverns, the palaces of fairies; a race of airy beings, who formed an intermediate class between men and demons, and who, if not positively malignant to humanity were yet to be avoided and feared, on account of their capricious, vindictive, and irritable dispositions. 'They ca' them,' said Mr Jarvie, in a whisper, 'Daoine Schie, whilk signifies, as I understand, men of peace; meaning thereby to make their gude-will. And we may as e'en as weel ca' them that too, Mr Osbaldistone, for there's nae gude in speaking ill o' the laird within his ain bounds."

Scott provides a long note to *Rob Roy* about 'Fairy Superstition' relating the story of Kirk's death as told by Patrick Graham. He also deals with Kirk in *Letters on Witchcraft and Demonology*, describing the district affectionately:

> "These beautiful and wild regions, comprehending so many lakes, rocks, sequestered valleys, and dim copsewoods, are not even yet quite abandoned by the fairies, who have resolutely maintained secure footing in a region so well suited for their residence."

Sir Walter Scott *Letters on Witchcraft and Demonology* 1830

Charles Nodier visited Scotland in June 1821 in company with Eugene Isabey, Alphonse de Cailleux and Baron Taylor, and wrote *Promenade de Dieppe aux montagnes d'Ecosse*. In 1822 the *Promenade* was translated into English, and published by Blackwood, Edinburgh. Like many other writers he admired Scott, and like Scott was interested in the supernatural. In his novel *Trilby*, set more in the vicinity of Loch Long and Inverary than the Trossachs, Nodier refers to a song, 'The Ghost of Aberfoyle', stated in a note to have been lost, and it is said that he based one of the characters on a boatman on Loch Katrine. In the *Promenade* there is a notable description of the ascent of Ben Lomond.

*

It is difficult to believe that **Jules Verne**, visiting Loch Katrine in 1859, would not have been told about the Loch Katrine aqueduct, the construction of which reached its culmination that year. Like every other visitor to the Trossachs, he also heard about the subterraneans, and about the fairy spirits which haunt the Trossachs. Verne mixed all this up and created a world in which Loch Katrine emptied itself into a huge underground cavern in his adventure story *Les Indes Noires*, The Black Diamonds. Verne was an enthusiastic admirer of Scott, and he lifts some passages from *Rob Roy* to lend verisimilitude to this adventure novel which was published in Britain as *The Child of the Cavern*. It describes an underground city hewn out of coal, and lit by electricity situated beneath the Trossachs. In the novel Verne points out 'Many superstitious beliefs exist both in the Highlands and Lowlands of Scotland... the Uruisk who more especially frequents the wild gorges of Loch Katrine.' Verne, who saw coalmines in Clackmannanshire, was mistaken in believing that the coal measures extended north of the Highland Line. However, the novel is very convincing of its kind, and it must be admired as a feat of the imagination. Verne's technique includes using a monster, the Sylfax, and using his knowledge of the mining industry to make the story a painless account of technicalities, but it is the underground city inhabited by 'subterraneans' which captures the imagination. He situates the 'Aberfoyle Mine', the entrance to this underground world, seven miles south-west of Callander. This, of course, is where Aberfoyle is, but Verne's topography is weak. The gothic entrance to the mine, however, owes much to the Glasgow Corporation:

> "Seven miles to the south west of Callander opened a slanting tunnel, adorned with a castellated entrance, turrets and battlements."
>
> Jules Verne *Les Indes Noires* 1877

Verne and his travelling companion, Hignard, visited Edinburgh, crossed the Forth to Fife, where they visited the caves at Wemyss, mentioned by Kirk; and then set out for Stirling, Bannockburn, Castlecary, and Glasgow. Thence they went to Balloch, and sailed up Loch Lomond to Inversnaid in the 'Prince Albert'. They crossed to Loch Katrine and the Trossachs. In the novel Verne has his hero and heroine make the same journey:

> "While breakfast was being prepared, Nell and her friends went to look at the waterfall which, from a considerable height, is precipitated into the loch, appearing just as if it had been put there as an ornament on purpose for the

> pleasure of the tourists. A suspension bridge spanned the tumultuous waters amidst clouds of spray. From this spot the eye surveyed the greater part of Loch Lomond …
>
> … Breakfast over, they made ready for the drive to Loch Katrine. At the Breadalbane Arms (it was the family of Breadalbane which promised to 'afford wood and water' to the fugitive Rob Roy) several comfortable carriages awaited the orders of travellers, affording all the convenience which distinguishes the coaching service of Great Britain. A splendid coachman in scarlet livery gathered up the reins of his four horses in his left hand, and the equipage began the ascent of the steep mountainside, the road following the windings of the bed of the torrent. As they ascended, the form of the mountain peaks seemed continually changing. On the opposite shores of the lake they rose with ever increasing grandeur, the heights of Arrochar overlooking the Inveruglas glen and Ben Lomond now exhibited the abrupt face of its northern side."

Verne stuffs the book with this kind of descriptive writing, and the action is brisk enough, but the novel, which is not one of his best efforts, is forgotten, although it has recently been reissued by Luath as *The Underground City* (2005), translated by Ian Thompson. The fantastic elements in the story, imaginative as they were, were not as spectacular as those in some of his other works, but it is a testimony to the fame of the Trossachs that they were the setting for this French romance.

*

Andrew Lang, folklorist, poet, novelist and historian had a great interest in Kirk, and wrote the introduction to *The Secret Commonwealth* of 1893. His academic work is considered unreliable and slapdash, and the text of his 1893 edition is very difficult to understand because of poor transliteration. Lang's dedication provides a further powerful literary connection. It is an amusing and neglected dialect poem addressed to Robert Louis Stevenson. RLS was then in Samoa, where he was known as 'Tusitala', said to mean 'teller-of-tales'. Stevenson was, of course, much interested in the Scottish church, in the Covenant, and in the weird and the supernatural. Stewart Sanderson connects Kirk with Stevenson in another way. Kirk describes the insubstantial nature of fairies' bodies, and the difficulty which therefore arises of, say, stabbing them. Sanderson goes on as follows:

> "Kirk says that the fairies' bodies are invulnerable, unlike the earthly bodies of witches and werewolves, which can be destroyed when their assumed astral bodies are elsewhere. This may recall to some readers Robert Louis Stevenson's tale of Tod Lapraik, the weaver in Catriona, when the hunters of solan geese

saw from their boat the great whirling shape dancing on the Bass Rock and shot a silver bullet at it; and at the very moment the bullet struck the apparition, Tod Lapraik's body collapsed over his loom in the cottage in North Berwick. This fine tale of the supernatural – one that stands rereading fully as well as the same author's Thrawn Janet – is surely one of the outstanding examples in any tongue of the transmuting of folk-belief into art literature."

R. B. Cunninghame Graham peopled his Scottish sketches with references to fairies, as the following extracts show:

"Hills towered and barred the north, and to the south the moors stretched until they met another range of hills, and all the space between them was filled with a great sea of moss, eyed here and there with dark black pools on which a growth of water-lilies floated like fairies' boats. A wooded hill, which sloped down to a brawling river, was the fairies court."

At Dalmary 1910

"A little river, in which, before the days of knowledge, kelpies were wont to live, flows past the town. Its glory is a pool (we call it linn) known as Linn-a-Hamish. Here the stream spreads out and babbling in its course wears the stones flat as proverbs in the current of men's speech get broadened out."

Salvagia 1899

"It is indeed a little hidden loch, lying so deep and unsuspected in its hollow between the hills that the first Celt or Pict who came upon it, ages ago, must straight have hit upon the name it bears. Nature seems, now and then, to have suspected that a time would come when all her secrets would lie bare and open to the prying eye of vulgar curiosity, and to have hid away some of her chiefest beauties in places where they are in sanctuary, hallowed from human gaze, which at the same time worships and violates them. So she set this little gem, remote, hiding it as a hind conceals her young, deep in the heather, underneath the tallest bracken and in a wilderness of hills. They tower on every side, bare bald and windswept, whilst in a corrie nestles the little lake, upon whose surface the wind scarcely or never preys, leaving it calm, mysterious, and unruffled, as if it held some secret, too natural for us to understand. If fairies still exist, they come, no doubt, from the Sith Bruach which guards the Avon Dhu at Aberfoyle, and sail their boats of acorn-cups and leaves on the black lakelet. Upon the little beach they run their craft ashore and dance on the broad ribbon of smooth sand which rings the lake, as a black mezzotint edged round with white. But if the fairies come, they come unseen, leaving no token

> of their passage but a few turned up leaves which they have used for boats, and the mysterious circlet of white foam in which float flies that have ventured further than their wings can bear them, and now wash up and down, as in some distant island of the South Seas drowned mariners may drift upon the beach."
>
> *Lochan Falloch* 1909

Another local author who wrote about fairies was **Henry Terrell** (fl.1935–54) who lived in Stirling. *The Wee Folk of Menteith* is a children's book, incorporating folk tales from Aberfoyle and elsewhere. Terrell also wrote a number of poems referring to Kirk.

*

A notable modern collector of oral folk tales was **R. MacDonald Robertson** (fl.1936–60), the author of several distinguished books about fishing in the Highlands. In *Selected Highland Folk Tales*, edited by Jeremy Bruce-Watt, he relates a macabre folk-tale about a water-monster in Loch Chon, the dog loch. The story is about the murder of a young boy by a tinker who threw the lad into the loch, where he was taken by a monster shaped like a dog. A more recent visitor to the spot had a vision of the same incident. Cunninghame Graham states that there is a kelpie in the Tinker's Loch, in the hills above Loch Chon. Whether it is the same one, or not, is not clear, but it seems likely. A further folk story from the district concerns the kelpie which haunts Loch Venachar. This seized some young children who bathed in the Loch. To this day the wood at this spot is called the wood of lamentation.

*

After the Doon Hill at Aberfoyle the most important fairy site in the Trossachs District is Coire nan Uruisgean on Ben Venue. It is said that it was given to the fairies by the Earl of Menteith to get them off his back. He was plagued by fairies, as is related elsewhere, at Inchmahome. The name is given in various forms and translated in various ways. Sometimes it appears as the "corrie of the satyrs", or, more poetically, the "den of the ghosts", or the "goblins' cave". They are all the same place. It appears most famously in *The Lady of the Lake*. Scott offers the following description in a note "This is the very steep and most romantic hollow in the mountain of Ben Venue, overhanging the south-western extremity of Loch Katrine. It is surrounded with stupendous rocks, and overshadowed with birch trees, mingled with oaks, the spontaneous production of the mountain, even where its cliffs appear denuded of soil."

In the poem it is the subject of one of Scott's most famous pieces of descriptive writing. He piles image on image in describing the mountain retreat where Ellen Douglas and her father hide:

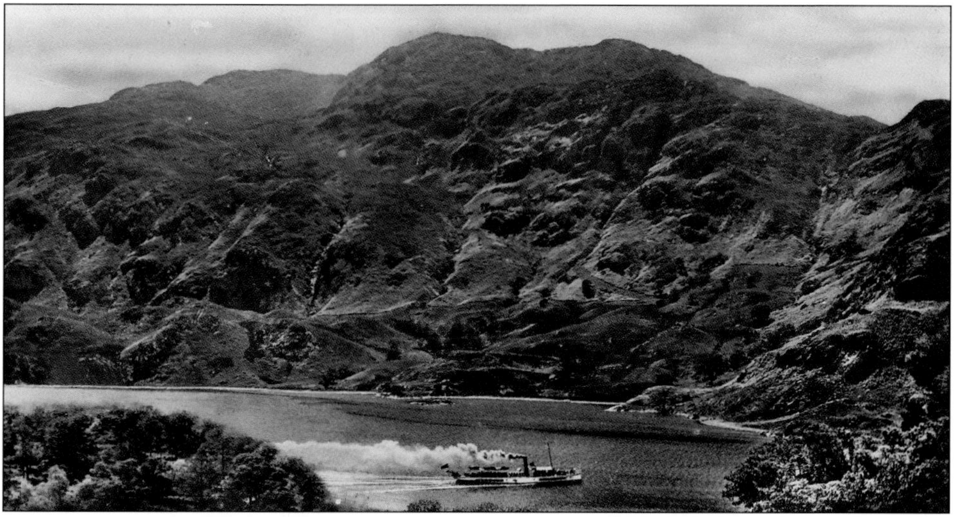

Ben Venue: Corrie nan Uruisgean is in the middle of the picture

It was a wild and strange retreat,
As e'er was trod by outlaw's feet.
The dell, upon the mountain's crest
Yawned like a gash on warrior's breast;
Its trench had staid full many a rock,
Hurled by primaeval, earthquake shock
From Ben Venue's gray summit wild,
And here, in random ruin piled,
They frowned incumbent o'er the spot
And formed the rugged sylvan grot.
The oak and birch, with mingled shade,
At noontide there a twilight made,
Unless when short and sudden shone
Some straggling beam on cliff or stone,
With such a glimpse as prophet's eye
Gains on thy depth, Futurity.
No murmur waked the solemn still,
Save the tinkling of a fountain rill;
But when the wind chafed with the lake,
A sullen sound would upward break,
With dashing hollow Voice, that spoke,
The incessant war of wave and rock.
Suspended cliffs with hideous sway
Seem'd nodding o'er the cavern gray.
From such a dell the wolf had sprung,
In such the wild-cat leaves her young;
Yet Douglas and his daughter fair
Sought for a space their safety there.
Gray Superstition's whisper dread
Debarr'd the spot to vulgar tread
For there she said did fays resort
And satyrs hold their sylvan court
By moonlight tread their mystic maze
And blast the rash beholder's gaze.

Glenfinlas is also associated with the supernatural and with Scott, who makes it the setting of a weird ballad, *Glenfinlas*, or *Lord Ronald's Coronach*, and he refers to it in *The Lady of the Lake* making it the setting of even weirder goings-on in that poem. Glenfinlas (or, Glenfinglas, the accepted spelling) caught Scott's imagination because it had, at the time he first visited it, both a magical name and a different appearance from the rest of the district. Whether this was on account of the fact that it had been preserved as a royal deer forest or not, is not clear, but both Patrick Graham and Alexander Campbell refer to the appearance of its greensward. Coleman Parsons summarises the plot of *Glenfinlas* as follows, alluding to its richness in superstition:

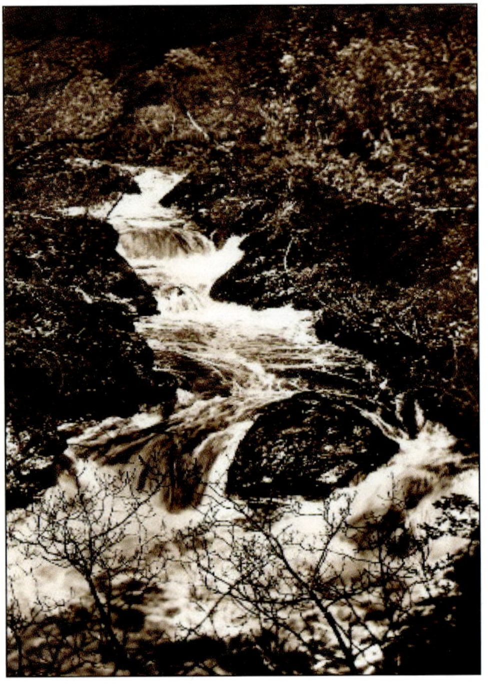

Glenfinlas

> "The action belongs to a time when red deer were hunted with bows and arrows, and the scene is near the poet's favourite Loch Katrine and Ben Ledi. Sheltered in a hut on a moonlit night, Lord Ronald longs for the presence of Glengyle's daughter, Mary. In spite of second sighted Moy's reporting death-damps on his friend's brow, corpse lights, and the cry of Ronald's warning spirit, the amorous chief descends a dell for a tryst with Mary. Later Moy refuses to let a green-clad huntress wile him out in search of the lovers. The spirit then expands horribly, a storm rips the hut apart, and fragments of Lord Ronald rain from the sky on his virtuous friend. The youth has been torn to bits by a succubus disguised as a wayward Lady of the Glen."

Witchcraft and Demonology in Scott's Fiction 1964

Scott says that since then Glenfinlas has been called 'the Glen of the Green Women'. In a note in *The Lady of the Lake* he elaborates on the significance of the colour green:

> "As the Daoine Shi', or Men of Peace, wore green habits, they were supposed to take offence when any mortals ventured to assume their favourite colour. Indeed, from some reason, perhaps originally a general superstition, green is held in Scotland to be particularly unlucky to particular tribes and counties. The Caithness men, who hold this belief, allege as a reason, that their bands wore that colour when they were cut off at the battle of Flodden; and for the same reason they avoid crossing the Ord on Monday, being the day of the week on which their ill-omened array set forth. Green is also disliked by those

> of the name of Ogilvy; but more especially it is held fatal to the whole clan of Graham. It is remembered of an aged gentleman of that name, that when his horse fell in a fox-chase, he accounted for it at once by observing, that the whipcord attached to his lash was of this unlucky colour."

Scott also makes Glenfinlas the site of a ritual to divine the future in Canto IV of *The Lady of the Lake* and provides the following note by way of explanation:

> "The Highlanders, like all rude people, had various superstitious modes of inquiring into futurity. One of the most noted was the Taghairn, mentioned in the text. A person was wrapped up in the skin of a newly slain bullock, and deposited beside a waterfall or at the bottom of a precipice, or in some other strange, wild, and unusual situation, where the scenery around him suggested nothing but subjects of horror. In this situation, he revolved in his mind the question proposed; and whatever was impressed upon him by his exalted imagination, passed for the inspiration of the disembodied spirits who haunt the desolate recesses."

The most recent novelist to visit Kirk is **James Robertson** (b. 1958). In his novel *The Testimony of Gideon Mack* (2006), Mack's father describes *The Secret Commonwealth* as "A curious book written by a curious man. I use the word curious in both its senses." Kirk is referred to again and he constitutes a leitmotif of the book.

One should not get the impression that all of the literature of the Trossachs is about fairies, but it can safely be said that Kirk certainly started something. His literary influence has extended well into the twenty-first century.

THE TOPOGRAPHY OF FAIRYLAND

> "The lakes and precipices amidst which the Avon-Dhu, or River Forth, has its birth, are still, according to popular tradition, haunted by Elfin people, the most peculiar, but most pleasing, of the creations of Celtic superstitions. "
>
> Walter Scott *Rob Roy* 1817

> "The semi-highland district with its wealth of billowy little hills, covered by scrubby oak, with now and then an old scotch fir clinging to an outcrop of rock, its trunk as red as a stripped cork tree in the Estremenian glades, was a fit setting for the fairy minister."
>
> R.B. Cunninghame Graham *The Secret Commonwealth* 1933

The visitor approaching Aberfoyle from Stirling or Callander will reach the Lake of Menteith first. On the southern shore of this loch there is a long narrow peninsula, Arnmach [NN 57 00], which stretches out in the direction of the island of Inchmahome. This peninsula is said to have been built by the fairies. It is said that the Earl of Menteith opened a Fairy Book and released them, and that they pestered him to give them work. They were given the task of making a rope of sand by the Earl. They tired of making the rope of sand and began to haunt him again, so he gave them Coire nan Uruisgean on Ben Venue as a gathering place. There is also a fairy hill called Bogle Knowe [NS 585 996] at the Lake of Menteith.

In Aberfoyle the visitor will want to see Robert Kirk's grave. This is reached from the Car Park in the village by crossing the old Brig o' Forth. A short distance down the road on the left-hand side is the cemetery and, just beyond it, the Old Kirk [NN 518 005]. The present ruin dates from 1774. Kirk's grave is beside the south-east corner of the building.

From the graveyard the Manse, re-built in the eighteenth century, can be seen and beyond it Doon Hill [NN 52 00]. This can be reached by the forest road to Gartmore. Forestry Commission signs point the way to a Nature Trail. This follows a track which weaves its way up the hill to the Minister's Pine at the summit. From the top of the hill it returns by a different route. The hill opposite is called the Fairy Knowe (a doppelganger for Doon Hill); the old Glasgow road winds over it to Gartmore.

There are two more modern churches in Aberfoyle. The Parish Church [NN 514 012] in Lochard Road, designed by John Honeyman, has a 'Boyle' Irish Bible. St Mary's Episcopal Church (1893–94) is in the village. It is, of course, this church, being Episcopalian, at which Kirk would have been a Minister.

Loch Chon, with its legendary water bull, is beside the road to Inversnaid. Lochan a'

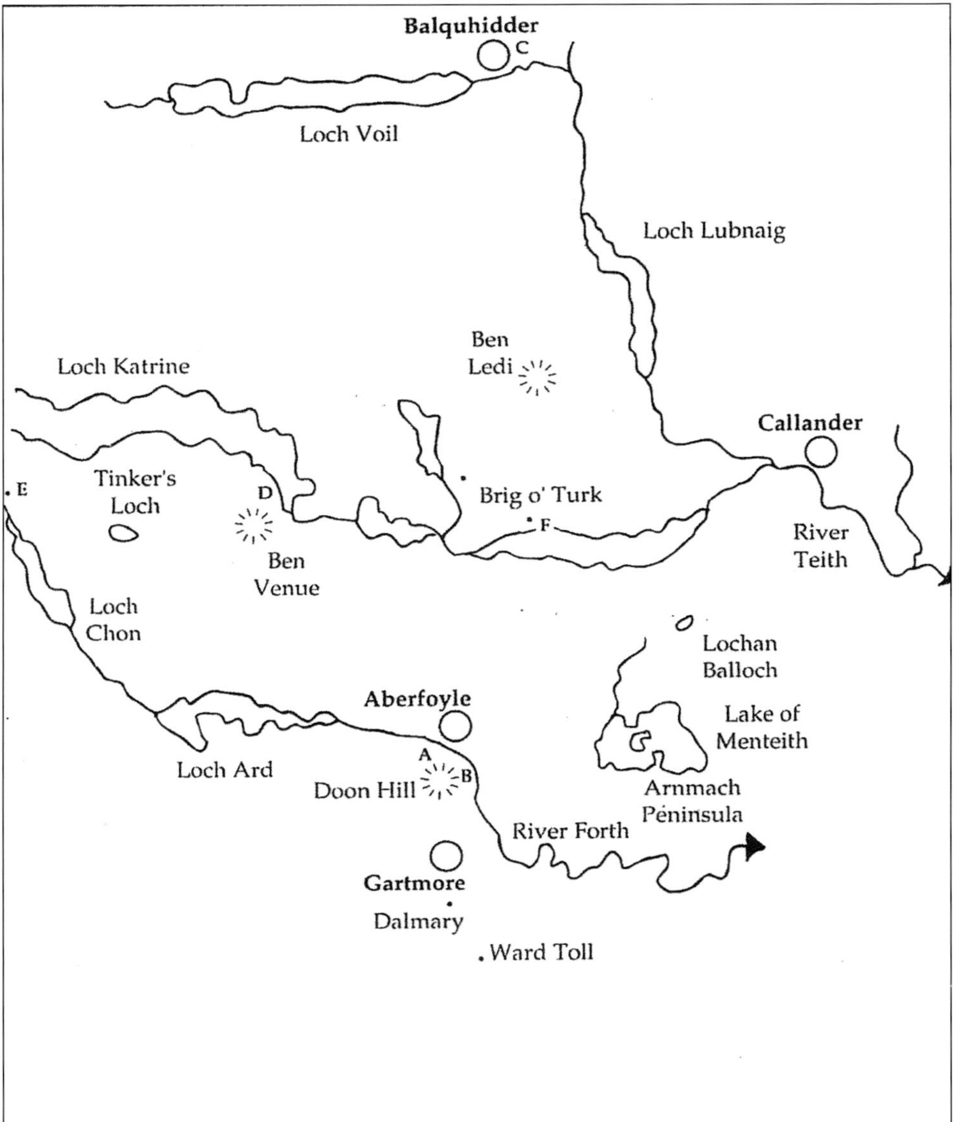

Fairy Sites in the Trossachs

A	*Robert Kirk's Grave*
B	*Minister's Pine*
C	*Balquhidder Kirk*
D	*Coire nan Uruisgean*
E	*Fairy Corrie*
F	*Wood of Lamentation*

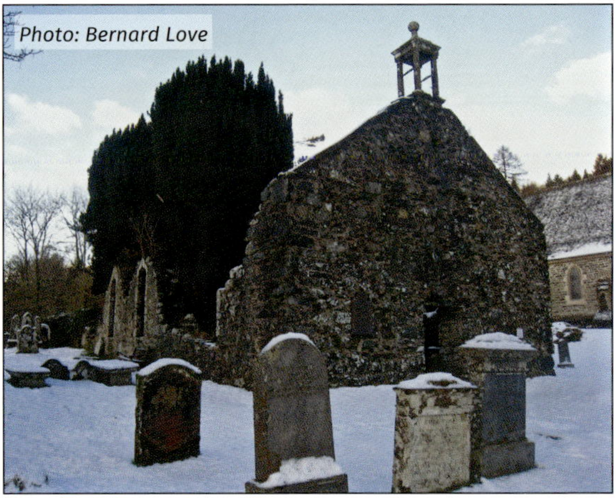

Old Church, Balquhidder

Chierd [NN 44 06], which is also said to be the haunt of a kelpie, and is now stocked with trout, is more difficult to reach. It is situated on the bleak moor between Ben Venue and Stronachlachar. Reaching it involves a difficult hill walk from Loch Chon which nevertheless commands good views.

Just beyond the head of Loch Chon beside the road, and where the Loch Katrine Aqueduct crosses it, there is another Fairy Hill [NN 411 079]. The mountain hollow which the Aqueduct traverses is Patrick Graham's Corrie of the Fairies. There is a pleasant circular walk from the corrie to Loch Katrine returning via the track which branches off from the Old Military Road.

Fairy sites in the Trossachs can be reached from either Callander or Aberfoyle. From Callander the road runs beside Loch Venachar. Just beyond Milton, where there are car parks beside the loch, Coille a' Bhroin, the wood of lamentation, marks the place where a kelpie is said to have carried off some local children.

Glenfinglas, the 'glen of the green women', has another Fairy Hill, Cnoc nan Sidheag [NN 533 071]. Scott's ballad *Glenfinlas* (1810) appeared in both *Tales of Wonder* and *Minstrelsy of the Scottish Border*:

All dropping wet her garments seem;
Chill'd was her cheek, her bosom bare,
As, bending o'er the dying gleam,
She wrung the moisture from her hair.
With maiden blush she softly said,
"O gentle huntsman, hast thou seen,
In deep Glenfinlas' moonlight glade
A lovely maid in vest of green?"

The tradition on which these stanzas are founded runs thus: while two Highland hunters were passing the night in a solitary bothy, and making merry over their venison and whisky, one of them expressed a wish that they had pretty lasses to complete their party. The words were scarcely uttered, when two beautiful young women, clothed in green, entered the hut, dancing and singing. One of the hunters was induced by one of the sirens to leave the hut; the other remained, and, suspicious of the fair seducers, continued to play on a Jew's harp, a strain, consecrated to the Virgin Mary. Day at length came, and the temptress vanished. Searching in the forest, he found the bones of his unfortunate friend, who had been torn to pieces and devoured by the fiend into whose toils he had fallen. The place was thence called the Glen of the Green Women.

At the foot of Loch Katrine is the heart of the Trossachs. Coire nan Uruisgean [NN 48 07], said to have been given to the uruisks by the Earls of Menteith to get rid of them, can be reached by a rough footpath from the Loch Achray Hotel or the Achray Car Park. It gradually rises above the foot of Loch Katrine to the Bealach nam Bo, the pass of the cattle, commanding very fine views.

A further important relatively local site is the parish church in Balquhidder [NN 535 209], best known as the burial place of Rob Roy.

This was where Kirk spent his first twenty years as minister. His first wife is buried there; her grave (Isabel Campbell) is at the top of the bank above the west gate of the churchyard. Kirk is said to have carved the inscription. In the church is the bell of the old church, dated 1684, and presented to the church by Kirk. In two glass cases there is, in one, a 'Boyle' Bible; and, in the other, an O'Donnell Gaelic New Testament, edited by Kirk.

A NOTE ABOUT RECENT DEVELOPMENTS ON DOON HILL

Recently (April, 2015) Stirling Council initiated a series of carvings at Doon Hill, Aberfoyle. These include various "fairy homes". The innovation makes a charming addition to the hill, but, regrettably perhaps, the fairies are clearly "tiny people" rather than the "alternatives to ourselves" that Kirk described. The fairy carvings are like the older "fairy doors" found near Minstead in the New Forest.

It should also be noted that the "clootie tree" at the top of the hill is recent and not part of any local tradition. Twenty-five years ago, local children occasionally made a wish at the Minister's Pine, perhaps leaving a small coin embedded in there or in a neighbouring tree. Now there are at least two trees laden with rags. A "cloot" is a strip of cloth or rag, and a "clootie well" is a well or spring, with an assortment of garments or rags left near it having been dipped in the well with the idea of rotting the cloth to bring about healing. A good example in Scotland is at Avoch in the Black Isle.

Current proposals include a trail from the village to the old Kirk and Doon Hill which will offer improved interpretation, and a wider understanding of Kirk. It is also hoped to assist in bringing about a more sensitive management of Doon Hill.

BIBLIOGRAPHY

Books

Black's Guide	*The Trossachs* (1853–1920)
Briggs, Katharine	*The Anatomy of Puck* (1965) *The Fairies in Tradition and Literature* (1967) *Dictionary of Fairies* (1976)
Chambers, Robert	*Domestic Annals of Scotland* (1858–61)
Graham, Patrick	*Sketches of Perthshire* (1806)
Graham, R.B. Cunninghame	*Doughty Deeds* (1925, Heinemann) *Notes on the District of Menteith* (1895, Black) *Scottish Stories* (1914, Duckworth)
Henderson, Lizanne & Cowan, Edward J.	*Scottish Fairy Belief* (2001, Dundurn)
Hunter, Michael	*The Occult Laboratory* (2001, Boydell & Brewer)
Kirk, Robert	*The Secret Commonwealth* (1691)
(edited Scott, (Sir)Walter)	*The Secret Commonwealth* (1815)
(edited Lang, Andrew)	*The Secret Commonwealth* (1893, Bibliothèque de Carabas)
(edited Sanderson, Stewart)	*The Secret Commonwealth* (1976, Folklore Society)
(edited Graham, R.B.C)	*The Secret Commonwealth* (1933, Aeneas MacKay)
Lang, Andrew	*Ban and Arrière Ban* (Poems) (1894)
MacGregor, Alasdair Alpin	*Somewhere in Scotland* (1935) *Land of the Mountain and the Flood* (1965)
McKerracher, Archie	*Perthshire in History and Legend* (1988, John Donald)
Nodier, Charles	*Promenade de Dieppe aux Montagnes d'Ecosse* (1822)
Parsons, Coleman	*Witchcraft and Demonology in Scott's Fiction* (1964)
Robertson, R. MacDonald	*Selected Highland Folk Tales* (1961, Oliver & Boyd)
Scott, Sir Walter	*Lady of the Lake* (1810) *Waverley* (1814) *Rob Roy* (1817) *Tales of a Grandfather* (1828–30) *Letters on Demonology and Witchcraft* (1830)
Spence, Lewis	*The Fairy Tradition in Britain* (1948, Rider & Co)

Stewart, R.J. — *Robert Kirk – Walker Between Worlds* (1990)
Stott, Louis — *Robert Kirk* (2002, Oxford Dictionary of National Biography)
Terrell, Henry — *The Wee Folk of Menteith* (1935, Stirling)
Walker John — *Scottish Sketches of Cunninghame Graham* (1982)
Wentz, W.Y. Evans — *The Fairy Faith in Celtic Countries* (1973, Lemma, NY)

Articles

Maclean, Donald — *The Life and Literary Labours of Rev Robert Kirk of Aberfoyle* (Trans. Gaelic Soc. Inverness, Vol 31, 1922–24)
Sanderson, Stewart — *A Prospect of Fairyland* (Folklore, Vol 75, 1964)
Spence, Lewis — *The Mystery of Robert Kirk* (Scots Magazine, Vol 43, 1945)